Women Arising

7 Ancient Secrets from Proverbs 31
for the Modern-Day Woman

Ellianna Temple &
Melissa McCray

Dedication:

This book is first dedicated to our Lord God, Father, Son and Holy Spirit who is the inspiration and motivation behind it; to the generation of modern-day women, our sisters, wanting to live the full and satisfied life to reach their highest potential as women of God; to our mother, Jo McCray, our aunt, Mary Maude Shafer, and both of our grandmothers, Virginia Bailey and Gloria Spearman; and to countless other women who have walked with us and taught us so much from their own examples and life choices.

Table of Contents

Trust: A Heart at Rest

Intentional Love All Your Days - Prayer and Action
Concerned with His Reputation
Get Your Finances Together, Together
Lead by Example: Couple Time
Health: Invest in the Best, Don't Shortcut Your Home
Hospitality: Serving Messy Oxen
Foresight: Foreseeing the Unseen
In tune with Home: Strong Water
Creating Memories
Exuding Wisdom: Become a Learner, a Reader, a Leader
Law of Kindness: It's in God's DNA
Teaching the Younger: Love is the Best Teacher
The Value of Toil and Reward
Income Contributor: Growing Wealth from Your Earnings
Quality Investments
Integrity: The Riches of Knowing Who You Are

A Note to the Reader

When we were children, our parents would go away every New Year's for a few days to celebrate their anniversary and to plan for the New Year. When they returned, they would encourage us to set our own goals for the New Year. They taught us that there are five categories that every person should set goals for and prioritize. Our new goals often included things like a new dog or doghouse and trips to Disneyland. As we grew into adulthood, we continued to set goals every new year. In this book, we've taken those five categories and added others that we've found in Proverbs 31 and outlined what a woman arising looks like.

We know we could talk about principles and guidelines all day. But nothing becomes more real than when you see it lived out in a person. We praise God. We have been blessed and privileged to have examples of Godly women who lived out the guidelines in Proverbs 31 that we will be covering. Through this book, we hope that you can partake in what we have received and participate in their wisdom with us. May this book be a mentor to you of the collected sayings, principles, and wisdom from the word of God and of the women we admire.

As our mother often said, "When you read a book, you are getting the wisdom and counsel of a person's entire life and hours and hours of work, similar to sitting down and having a cup of coffee with them." We desire you to have this same kind of relationship with us — just like we were sitting down and getting coffee together as girlfriends, sharing thoughts and experiences we have learned. We feel that even by you purchasing this book and investing your time to read it, we have already entered into a relationship with each other.

Preface

Woman Arising — what does that look like? Women who rise up to their God-given destiny and calling according to Scripture is the crux of this book. Culture puts its own ceiling and definition of what a powerful woman looks like. We want to raise the bar for our generation to rise up from that limited definition put on them by culture and break into who they are really destined to be by God!

This book is designed for the modern-day woman who is trying to discern and determine her identity and priorities in life. It sculpts the image of this woman who arises, and it strives to answer that question, irrespective of whether the woman is single, dating, engaged or married. This book will help you prioritize your life into seven major categories/priorities. We will determine what this woman looks like and how she lives her life. In today's world, she can look like almost anything. When opportunities for women are basically limitless, she can be defined by whatever she wants: athlete, soldier, mom, businesswoman, CEO, entrepreneur, etc. The woman described in Proverbs 31 did it all. She tended to her home, had several businesses, and honored her husband and God, all while ministering to her children and the poor. Sound like a superwoman? No, she just knew how to prioritize her life.

Some may view living by priorities as limiting; but for the Proverbs 31 woman, it was liberating. We too, to be a woman arising, must choose to live by these priorities. This book does not limit women but gives them wings to take flight and to define their beauty and glory through every facet of their arising. Many things in today's culture pull at women to be the impossible and to look a certain way. This book will take you back to the basics. Don't try to be the perfect mom, wife or woman. Live life through the lens of Proverbs 31, and you'll find yourself fulfilled in living out your calling as the woman God designed you to be.

They say you can't have it all. However, the Proverbs 31 women certainly seemed to. This book outlines the seven secrets to a woman's fulfilled and enriched life. The priorities outlined in Proverbs 31 apply to every woman, every career and every path of life. God lays out a plan. Now it's up to us to live that out and build our own uniquely designed spiritual houses. Join us in the journey of *Women Arising*, step into your own arising and soar.

Secret I - God

Chapter 1
First Things First: Beauty Revealed

"Charm is deceptive, and beauty is fleeting; but a woman who fears the Lord is to be praised." (Prov. 31:30 NIV)

"Seek ye first the kingdom of God and His righteousness and all these things will be added to you." (Matthew 6:33 KJV)

The first and most important priority for any woman (or human being, for that matter) is our relationship with God. Our relationship with God is the bedrock of our lives — the foundation from which all other areas of life stem. When we understand who we were designed to be and how the Father sees us, then we can truly step into our identity as a daughter of the King. It's all about identity: knowing our purpose as women and knowing how the Father sees us is at the core of understanding our identity. If we want a strong and powerful relationship with Him, we have to understand how He sees us and understand the purpose for which women were created.

We're going to share a hard truth that you may not like. It's not popular because it involves dying to self, but it's the truth and must be stated at the beginning of this book. This truth is the foundation, heart and thesis and it is this: the virtuous woman knows her purpose in life, which is the foundation for her attitude and actions. She knows she was designed for a purpose, to be a helper, even before sin was in the world (Gen 2:18). Women were made to help. We help our husbands. We help at work. We help at home. We help in our communities. We help. She approaches life every day with the intent of being a daughter of the King, virtuous wife to her husband or virtuous woman to humankind, mother to her children, keeper of her home or domain, and a woman of impact in whatever sphere of influence she has, whether in business, ministry, community or beyond. Understand this and you understand the bedrock this book is built upon. Understand this and you understand half of your identity as a woman.

In addition to knowing our role as a helper, we have to define what beauty is in order to get a full picture of our identity. An understanding of beauty is at the core of who a woman is because most women get validation from their understanding of beauty. Beauty is what lies deep within us and radiates outward to grace our face.

Let's look at it like this: if we have a problem in our lives, it is most likely due to a problem in our spiritual lives. Often what happens in the spiritual realm manifests in the physical. We remember, as little girls, hearing our dad tell a story of a couple who was having a hard time in their marriage. With marital fighting at its height, they decided to inform their pastor of their problems and invite him over to help counsel them. The doorbell rang and the husband (we'll call him Jim) answered the door and invited the pastor into the living room to discuss their problems. As they sat down, the pastor asked, "Jim, how's your relationship with the Lord coming along? Describe that to me." Jim was surprised by the question because he fully expected the pastor to ask about their marriage and discuss what they needed to do to make things right. As children, this story had a profound impact on how we viewed problems in our lives. If something is off in your life or if you are struggling, that's a good indicator that you should return to the feet of Jesus and get things settled in your heart, much in the same way that when we as women find we are getting out of rest or feeling anxious, we have to go back to our identity in who Jesus made us to be: women who are fully known and loved by the Father — not because of what we do but because of who He made us to be. He sees us much in the same way He sees the Holy Spirit. Jesus said, "I give you the Holy Spirit to come after me as a 'helper,'" (John 14:26) which is the same word described for a woman. Women have much the same purpose as the Holy Spirit: to help. That's our identity. We are who He says we are. We are a tender voice and an impression on the world — guiding others to Christ through our actions and what we believe. Yet, at times, much like the Holy Spirit, we can be strong and warrior-like. Learn to listen to and understand the Holy Spirit and you'll better understand your true identity.

In the story above, Jim was surprised to be asked about his relationship with God when it was his relationship with his wife that needed help.

Yet, when we experience pain in our body, such as a headache, sore muscles, cramps etc., it lets us know something is not right. In the same way, marital issues, self-esteem issues, feeling guilty, fighting, etc. are also symptoms that let us know something is not right between us and the Lord. (James 4:1). Press into your identity and you'll see a new creature emerge, walking in boldness and calm confidence. Knowing who you are as a daughter first, will help you know who you are as a child second.

Ellianna: Back to beauty: for a time, I worked in the modeling world and I can't tell you how many conversations I overheard where male models referred to female models as "ugly" because they were acting like "B*tches." As I listened to them talking, I realized how fleeting outer beauty is. Men may be attracted to a beautiful woman for a time, but what is truly beautiful to men of her personhood and of her heart. God is so amazing, unlike humans, he is not distracted by a dangling carrot of outer beauty because he sees right into our heart. He sees our values and our inner beauty. He knows us so intimately. He designed and fashioned each of us after his own beauty because we are made in God's image. I would argue, therefore, that if we call ourselves ugly then we are in essence calling God ugly. Because we are, after all, made in His image- designed for His glory. I get it. Having spent a year in the local modeling world with runway shows and fashion, I saw how easy it was to get wrapped up in the world's definition of beauty as all-encompassing. While adorning ourselves and looking pretty makes us feel good, we have to ask ourselves, "who are we doing it for? Am I adorning myself for God's glory and honor?" As a woman, I think it's our unique design to show the world a picture of true beauty by how we dress and how we act. But if the definition of beauty stops there, then we have missed the mark. God's definition of beauty is so much deeper than outer appearance.

God gives us a beautiful story in the Bible to help us understand how He sees beauty. Remember the story of how God instructed the prophet Samuel to find Israel's next king? God told Samuel to go to the house of Jesse, who had eight sons. One of them was David, the chosen one out of many brothers to be the next king. Samuel looked at the oldest, tallest and more outstanding brothers first thinking surely one of them was the chosen. But the Lord said to Samuel, "Do not look at his appearance or at his physical stature, because I have refused him. For the Lord does not see as man sees; for man looks at the outward appearance, but the Lord looks at the heart." (1 Samuel 16:7 NKJV) Then Samuel asked Jesse if he had any more sons. Jesse answered, "Yes." The youngest one, David, was sent for and came before Samuel and the Lord confirmed he was the chosen one to be anointed as Israel's next king.

Have you ever heard someone argue that the most beautiful thing to behold is the female body? It's interesting that God created woman last. Most artists' best and finest works, valued above all others, are toward the end of their careers after they've spent their lives perfecting their craft. Therefore, since Eve was created after Adam, could it be argued that God saved his best artwork for last?

To know our self-worth and value before the Lord, it's imperative we know our definition of beauty. That's why we wanted to affirm that you are beautifully designed because you are made in the image of God. If God saved His best art for last by creating woman, then it would stand to reason that Satan, being the most beautiful in Heaven ("...*You [Satan] were the seal of perfection, full of wisdom and perfect in beauty*" Ezekiel 28:12 NIV), would hate women — because we stole his thunder. Choose any time in history to take a quick look at the overall treatment of women, rather from the Roman Empire era when females babies were left to die on the streets, to current day China where female babies are often aborted simply because they are not male offspring. Yes, take your pick of any time throughout history and women have been degraded in various ways: sold into sex trafficking, devalued at birth, denied education and become victims of domestic violence. One can only imagine how this grieves the heart of God.

Knowing the enemy's tactics and strategy is halfway to defeating him. Once we know who we are and define our beauty and worth, we can more effectively develop our relationship with God. If He is the definition of beauty and we are made in His image, then by default, we ourselves are beautiful. We have the liberty to walk in freedom knowing we are beautiful and fearfully made. There is no room for self-condemnation because we are His children.

Any beauty we have, whether physical or in the heart, is given to point others to Christ. The definition of true beauty, just like Satan's beauty, was originally meant to reflect the glory of God. In Satan's rebellion, he became jealous of God's glory, beauty and majesty and wanted to use his own beauty for his personal praise. This attitude of self-worship allowed evil to enter the world and sin crept in, attempting to steal God's glory, making people lovers of self instead of fearing God. Satan fell into the trap of self-worship, focusing on his own beauty instead of worshiping God and focusing on God's beauty. In the same way, women (because we are designed to represent God's beauty even as Satan was) are often more susceptible to fall into this trap also, trying to use our own beauty for self-worship for our own self-glorification rather than using the body (God's temple) to glorify Him. It's a fine line between being concerned with how we look because we're self-centered and being concerned with our looks because we want to reflect Christ. If Satan can keep us focused on ourselves and enamored with the few pounds we lost or gained, or the new pimples or wrinkles, then we are helping Satan in his agenda to steal the focus from God and in so doing, worshiping not God, but Satan. Again, it's a fine line. We want you to be concerned with how you look, but what's your motive?

So, how do we become a Proverbs 31 woman who fears the Lord? *"Charm is deceptive, and beauty is fleeting; but a woman who fears the Lord is to be praised."* (Proverbs 31:30 KJV)

We cannot fear God without first knowing who He is and in turn understanding who we are as a result. If we told you a man died for you and you didn't understand why or know who he was or his love for you, it wouldn't really mean much to you. But to fear God, we need to know who He is. We all want to be praised, but if fear of God is a prerequisite to being praised, what does it mean to fear God? The Bible tells us that the fear of the Lord is the beginning of wisdom. In fact, wisdom is one of the main attributes of a woman who fears the Lord. So, it's no surprise that the Bible says: a woman who fears God will be praised. Fear is a reverence of who God is and, indeed, it is very similar to respect and honor. Fear of God is valued and cherished and those who can obtain it shall be praised. All we have to do is ask as the apostle James reminds us, "If any of you lacks wisdom, you should ask God, who gives generously to all without finding fault, and it will be given to you." (James 1:5 KJV)

You mean that's it? All I have to do is ask and I can have wisdom? Yup, it's pretty clearly laid out for you in the Bible. However, not so with beauty; you may be praised for a time (in your youth), but beauty is deceptive because it is only surface deep and then it fades with time. Physical beauty is not long-lasting unlike the fear of the Lord which is eternal beauty because it's founded on something that never changes: the character of God. For He is the same yesterday, today and forever (Hebrews 13:8). God gives a definition of beauty, which is Himself, right there for women; and because we are made in His image that gives us eternal, everlasting beauty and because He designed us for a purpose: to glorify Him as a helper, we can now approach God in reverence and in fear knowing who He has called us to be: beautiful helpers, much like the Holy Spirit.

If you've never dedicated your body, His temple, and your beauty to God, we'd like to ask you to join us in dedicating your beauty to Him so that you won't fall into the same trap that Satan did. Please read the prayer below aloud as a declaration and proclamation.

Personal Beauty Dedication Prayer:

Dear Heavenly Father,

Thank you for the body and beauty that you have given me and sharing your beauty with me. I thank you for every stretch mark, roll of fat and imperfection on my skin. I thank You for helping me grow in the grace of knowing how to care and tend for this temple for Your glory. I refuse to use my beauty for self-worship or to get the eyes of the world to look at me, but rather to glorify You. I ask you to let my beauty, inward and outward, point the eyes of all who see me, to worship You and to see the beauty of the One whose image I bear. I align myself with Your word and acknowledge and declare in the face of the enemy that I am fearfully and wonderfully made in the image of God. Therefore, I declare and profess that I am beautiful. I will choose to honor what You have given me and not treat the temple of the Holy Spirit lightly, but with honor and reverence and walk worthy according to the manner of your calling in both health and diet. (Eph 4:1 NASV) I thank you for the bodily temple you have given me to house my spirit and Your Holy Spirit. Thank you for endowing me with your image. Help me to recognize every time I have self-degrading thoughts, to recognize them as from the enemy as his tactic is to worship the self instead of worshipping You. God, you are beautiful, and I am beautiful because you made me. By the grace of God, I propose and commit from this day forward to honor and glorify you through the beauty you have bestowed upon me. I trust You to lead and guide me to do this according to Your word and the leading of Your Spirit. I will not condemn myself or put myself down but walk in a meek and quiet spirit which are beautiful and precious to You. (1 Peter 3:4)

In Jesus' name, Amen.

Signature:_____

Date:_____

Chapter 2
Word of God

"For the word of God is alive and active. Sharper than any double-edged sword, it penetrates even to dividing soul and spirit, joints and marrow; it judges the thoughts and attitudes of the heart." (Hebrews 4:12 NIV)

Our mother, wise as she is, will be the first to tell you she has gotten her wisdom straight from the word of God along with the wise words of her mother and grandmothers and many other teachers of the Bible. In fact, one of her favorite quotes is: "Let books be your counselors and teachers and learn from the mistakes of others." However, the number one book she admonished us to read was the Bible: the source of all truth.

The word of God is like a road map for success, a blueprint for life, handcrafted by God Himself, making it supernatural. So, when we engage with the word of God, we are engaging with God himself.

"In the beginning was the Word, and the Word was with God, and the Word was God...The Word became flesh and made his dwelling among us." (John 1:1,14 NIV) Although the Word in this verse refers to Jesus the person, Jesus was Himself the fulfillment of the word of God of things spoken of in the Old Testament. Jesus' coming fulfilled the words God had spoken about Himself, His Son.

Our relationship with God is not just a cold, unfamiliar blueprint on a piece of paper giving us guidelines on how to build our lives. God is a real person with thoughts, feelings and emotions. So, the word of God is more than a blueprint for success: it's also a love letter to humankind. But because of His love and His desire for us to have success in all things, He uses His love letter like a concrete road map, giving us directions to live an abundant life. We could use an architect's blueprint without a personal relationship with the architect and still build a strong, solid house simply by following the design. But any builder will tell you the building of the house goes a lot smoother when there is access to the architect.

> Ellianna: My husband, Ben, works with lots of builders, designers and architects on many projects, and he tells me it's almost impossible to manage a project without having access to the designers, builders and architects. Because, during the building process, there are inevitable questions that come up that require access to the architect. The word of God is like that. Whether you're a Christian or not, you will have success if you follow the principles and blueprints outlined in God's word, just like any builder will have success following the architect's blueprint, but greater success is had when we have a personal relationship with the architect: God.

God wants us to not *just* use His principles for success, but really know and engage Him personally. This is actually the foundational truth to all the other truths, or principles, in the blueprint. You could say it's like the foundation. Without that foundation of a relationship, there's really no success, just like without a solid foundation, a house won't be strong and stable. We can build a house; it might be successful, but it won't be strong. Jesus explains this concept in a parable in Matthew 7:24-27. Two men set out to build a house. One builds his house on sand and the other builds on rock. When the winds and rain came, the house on the sand collapsed and the man lost everything. But the man whose house was built on the rock stood firm, despite the storm. The same is true with us. A relationship with God is like building our house on a solid foundation of rock. It will last despite the rain and strong wind. So, when life throws hardships at us, we will not stumble and fall because our lives are built on the foundation of God's word. And we must think of the word of God like food. It's something we need on a daily basis. (Matt 4:4 Deut. 8:3)

Starting off with a Bible reading plan helps get us reading the Word. We don't always have to stick to the plan, but just reading His word daily will transform you, guaranteed. Every time we read His word and learn more about Him, it's like a grand adventure of learning more about this God who loves us. If you're in love, you want to learn and know the person you're in love with; in the same way, the more we fall in love with God, the more our desire for His word grows within us.

Here is a list of practices that help foster and develop your relationship with God:

We encourage you to get on a regular Bible reading plan. Perhaps reading through the book *What The Bible Is All About* by Henrietta Jones is a good place to start. When we focus on God daily, it leaves little room for self-worship because the word of God pushes self away and lifts God high. Below are some different things that strengthen our relationship with Him.

- Reading the Bible
- Worshipping Him
- Prayer
- Fasting
- Journaling
- Intentional time with God
- Listening for Him to speak
- Acts of service

Melissa: I used to read the word as a child before I really had fallen in love with God. I was doing a "read through the Bible in a Year" reading plan. But then, when I fell in love with Him, it was like I had to read His word all the time and know about this One who loved me so much. Before, I just wanted to read the allotted portion of daily reading on my plan; but after falling in love with God, I just wanted to read more than the daily portion. What woman doesn't want to read a love letter/text every day from her boyfriend/husband/fiancé? The love letter can be short or long. But just the fact of having one every day keeps that love fresh. I could receive a daily love letter and then simply choose not to read it. God desires to open up more of His love to us daily but we actually must physically open the letter and read it. If I choose not to read it, then communication isn't really happening. So, we approach the word of God not only as a direction map for life and a blueprint for success but also as a love letter in which to be romanced by Him. In a marriage, a husband and wife could be very productive with goal setting and even accomplishing those goals. But if they have fallen "out of love" with each other, accomplishing their goals together has lost its beauty and joy.

Ellianna: Sometimes I don't always have the emotions of loving my husband. Sometimes I get frustrated with him because I don't get what I want, and the feelings of cuddly warmth aren't there. When he's singing loud in the morning, I tend to feel irritated. Yet, I choose to love him in those moments because love is something much deeper than a feeling; love is a choice. The same is true for our relationship with God. I may not always feel like spending time with God or reading His word, but because I truly, deeply love Him, I choose to read and spend time with Him. It's a choice that I decide to make. And, often, once we choose to act, our emotions will follow. On occasion, my husband, Ben, has traveled away for weeks at a time. When he's gone, my heart aches for his return. He typically will leave me love letters telling me how he feels and what he misses about me. I have to tell you, I read them over and over again and it never gets old. The same is true with us and God. Even though we've read His word before, because we long to be with Him, we long to read what He's written to us in His word... especially when we're feeling far apart from Him.

Make spending time with God like a date, a real appointment with a person. Tell God you want to meet with Him at a certain time every day/week, at a certain place. Many couples put their date night on their calendars to make sure they get time each week to connect. This way, they both know they can count on that time. Even successful business people say, "If it's not on your calendar, it won't get done." Time-blocking is so important if you want to make a habit of something. We encourage you to be of the same mindset with your time with the Lord. You're a lot more likely to achieve it if it's time-blocked on your schedule and life calendar.

> Melissa: I read a small little book called *Quiet Time: A Practical Guide for Daily Devotion*" (author unknown) that explained this concept to me. I set the time and place and just showed up for my date/appointment with God. Just like in real life, every date you go on can be different, but you're committed to show up and be there.

A date can involve different things. Here are some things we like to include in our special times with God:

Worship: we often sing songs of worship, Prayer: talking with God. Journaling, fasting and even walking in nature and admiring His creation can all be ways to draw close to God.

Chapter 3
Worship: Beholding His Worth

"In a loud voice they were saying: 'Worthy is the Lamb, who was slain, to receive power and wealth and wisdom and strength and honor and glory and praise!'"
(Revelation 5:12 NIV)

We love to worship. We grew up having worship time with our family every evening. Our dad plays the guitar and piano. So, after we had our family devotions, we would often break into song and music. As children, this was one of our favorite times because after sitting still while the Bible was read, we were ready to get up, dance, move around and shout. As people get older, their worship can become more reserved. They may not dance with the freedom they had as a child because they tend to worry about what others think. "And he said: 'Truly I tell you, unless you change and become like little children, you will never enter the kingdom of heaven.'" (Matt. 18:3 NIV)

But we know that God delights when we worship without reservation. We must be like little children and have that sense of abandonment of ourselves to truly worship, having the same spirit of King David who worshipped joyfully before the Lord when the Ark was brought back to Jerusalem. (2 Samuel 6) This is the same kind of unashamed excitement a little child shows when they see their mom or dad. Why are we so comfortable to dance in an exercise class or at a wedding, or even jump and scream during a football game but so reserved to give that same adoration, enthusiasm or praise to God?

To truly have a heart like David, to truly worship the King of Kings, we must enter into childlikeness — not childishness which is foolishness but childlikeness which is a complete focus on something other than what others think about us. We love watching children worship God. There is such an abandonment that we long to emulate. We have all heard people say "I don't sing" or "I don't play any instruments" as an excuse to not participate in communal or private worship. Did you know you don't have to do any of that when you worship? In the Old Testament, the word "praise" in Hebrew has seven different variations that describe worship and God delights to accept them all.

1. Barak (baw-rak')–to bow down to or kneel before the Lord.

Have you ever been in worship and found yourself moving from a standing or sitting position to one of kneeling? Sometimes this is such a comfortable place to be — on our knees before the king — speechless. Sometimes worship isn't about making noise, but just being still and knowing that He is God. (Zech 2:13, Ps 46:10)

2. Halal (haw-lal')–to shine, boast, rave about, celebrate or even to be clamorously foolish.

Whenever we boast about the Lord, we are worshiping him. Whenever we celebrate things important to him, we are worshiping him. Whenever we are "clamorously foolish," like in song or dance, we are worshiping him. This one reminds us of David because although his wife thought he looked foolish when he was dancing, the Lord loved it. Think about it. Has someone who loves you done something that appeared foolish to others simply because they loved you?

3. Shabach (shaw-bakh')–to shout loudly or command.

The Lord loves a good shout. (Ps 98) Shouting to God is a form of praise. You don't have to know how to sing or how to play an instrument or how to dance. Just shout and give a command while you're doing it. Command goodness over certain situations, and you are praising God. (Joshua 6)

4. Tehillah (teh-hil-law')–to sing unrehearsed, unplanned praises.

We love when this happens. We can recall a few moments with a group of friends when this happened, and it was powerful. We were traveling in Israel with some college friends for a mission trip and we entered a church, and someone broke out singing a hymn. Others joined in with different harmonies and melodies and then the hymn turned into a song we had never heard before. It was not a hymn, it was just people singing praises to God. And you know what? It all sounded in harmony and in sync. It sounded like we were in heaven. In fact, several other people who entered the church said it sounded like there were literally angelic angels who had joined in. This is perhaps some of the sweetest and purest praise because it's not rehearsed; it is from the heart and it is sincere.

5. Towdah (to-daw')–to extend or raise your hands in thanksgiving for something that hasn't yet occurred or that you haven't yet received.

This is faith in action. Again, if you "don't sing or play an instrument" this is your form of worship. Just lift your hands during worship and in your heart and mind, thank God for all he's going to do for you. Thank Him for things that haven't yet happened. This is praise! It's almost like you're putting your hands out — ready to receive and thank God in faith for things he's already given or thank Him for things He's already done. Again, the physical is a manifestation of what's in the heart. Tell your body to follow what your heart, soul and mind believe. It's no wonder God tells us to lay hands on the sick so they can receive healing (Mark 16:18). He doesn't just instruct us to pray but to express by the laying on of hands, or in this case, the raising of hands.

6. Yadah (yaw-daw')–to extend your hands vigorously as in complete surrender.

This is a good picture. Think of someone who is surrendering at gunpoint. This is the attitude we can have during worship. The act of raising your hands is an outward sign of your complete trust in the One and only King and the fact that He is God and you are not. It's an outward physical manifestation of what our heart's cry is. We often do this when we're praying or singing a song where surrender and/or adoration is evident.

7. Zamar (zaw-mar')–to touch the strings, mostly rejoicing.

Anytime you play an instrument in worship, especially when you're rejoicing over the King, this is worship. For all those musicians and singers, your voice, your musical instrument, is your form of praise.

The next time you worship, practice one of these variations of worship and see if you walk into a new realm of intimacy and freedom. Have the attitude of a child the next time you worship and see God take you to a new level of intimacy (In-to-ME-see). But even if you don't dance yet or have never learned to play an instrument or to sing, just start with worshipping from your heart - *love*. It's heart worship that God desires from you. So just begin bringing your heart to Him and the expressions will follow as you'll become so full of God's love that you won't be able to hold back expressing to Him. Be like a little child who loudly sings "Happy Birthday" off-key to their dad — unaware of how far from perfect they're singing but reveling in love and joy. We often find ourselves expressing this when we're alone in our cars where no one can hear.

"And let them sacrifice the sacrifices of thanksgiving, and declare his works with rejoicing." (Ps 107:22)

Worship begins at home. As Proverbs 31 women, we are to be cognizant and sensitive to the atmosphere and focus of our home. In our positions as wives and mothers, and even single ladies, we have the powerful position of influence and authority to set the tone in our home. Be creative in how to encourage and foster an attitude of worship in your home for your family and guests, or even if you're single and living on your own.

Some people say worship can't be taught, it's caught. Our opinion is that it's both/and not either/or.

If you've never danced before the Lord, the privacy of your own bedroom is a good place to start. Don't get so caught up with the different kinds of worship. Simply worship the Lord from your heart and be open to new and different expressions of adoration and worship to Him. It can be helpful to think of worship as one of two ways: be willing to be like little children before the high and exalted God and stand in awe and amazement of Him, even being silent before Him. The Lord says to be still and know that He is God. (Psalm 46:10) Some people have said the deepest kind of worship is when you have been brought to a place of total silence before Him, no word or action being sufficient in His presence.

The other way to look at worship is approaching it as a lover, as a bride of Christ. God often chooses a physical representation to illustrate a spiritual concept. For example, He gives us the picture of Him being our bridegroom and we being the bride — much in the same way we believe worship is a place of deep intimacy, much like a husband and wife coming together. How glorious it is that the Father invites us into deep fellowship and intimacy with Him on a continual basis through worship.

Two people come together, completely vulnerable and exposed, to love each other — no pretense. If you've ever had the great joy of truly being loved, you know that true loving relations can bring tears of joy and an overwhelming sense of intimacy. Worship, in the same way, breeds intimacy and a by-product can be tears of joy. In most healthy relationships that involve two lovers, you'll see a willingness to try new things, out of love for their partner. Even though it may be stepping into new territory and you may feel self-conscious, love is the willingness to try, the desire to give and not just to take.

As we "try" new and unchartered territories of worship, we may find ourselves feeling uncomfortable, but the end result — intimacy, is worth any forbearance on our part. Try out the 7 ways of worshiping God and see your relationship grow in passion and intimacy with the Lord. Worship is for the Lord and is unto Him. When we worship, with our focus and eyes on Him, we more easily move into forgetting ourselves and stop focusing on other people around us. We are then free to truly give to the Lord and focus on His worthiness and worship Him, and not by being self-conscious and worshiping ourselves by holding back praise and honor and worship to the only One worthy. Approach worship with the attitude of: "How can I bless You today, Lord?" As a byproduct of that act of worship, we, in turn, are ministered to when we worship in spirit and in truth. Worship (intimacy) is the purpose and reason for our existence. Or in other words, like the Westminster Shorter Catechism says, "The chief end of man is to glorify God and enjoy Him forever."

Grow deeper as a worshiper yourself and your home will be a mirrored heaven on Earth. Heaven has 24/7 worship going on before the throne of God with the 24 elders declaring the worship and glory of God and bowing down before Him. They never stop the cycle of beholding Him, declaring His majesty and bowing down before Him. Our lives and home are to be a constant ebb and flow of the heavenly dynamic. Jesus cares more about our everyday lives than any of us ever could. He'll lead each and every one of us into creating a place where the divine and holy meet the everyday and ordinary. Through the doors of worship, he'll take you to new heights of romance and intimacy.

Chapter 4
Prayer - Conversation with God

"Then the LORD God called to the man, 'Where are you?'"

(Genesis 3:9 NLT)

Prayer is mentioned over 600 times in the Bible (depending on what translation you use). There are many different kinds of prayers and ways of praying — beyond the scope of this book. So, we will just give a brief overview.

"If ye abide in me, and my words abide in you, ye shall ask what ye will, and it shall be done unto you." (John 15:7 KJV) A lot of people read over the first part of this verse and forget the if/then clause. *If* His words abide in *you then* you shall ask whatever you wish and it *shall* be granted. As we are in God's word, our desires change and conform more to His perfect will. You cannot have one without the other. A very good book on prayer that has had a huge impact on many across the world is *Intercessory Prayer* by Dutch Sheets. As a Greek scholar, Dutch not only shares from his own personal testimony with intercession, but also strongly supports its power and teaching from Scripture.

Prayer pushes back Satan's kingdom and builds up God's kingdom. As women, we often tend to be more in tune with the heartbeat of our homes than men are. Therefore, as women, we have a unique look into how to pray over and for our homes and families. Do we want to overcome Satan? Then we do so by the blood of the lamb and the word of our testimony (Rev. 12:11). Our testimonies are not only the truth of what God has done for us at the cross but also the stories of answered prayer and what God has done for us and for others — which are the byproduct of His finished work on Calvary. Do you want to beat the battle between you and Satan? Pray and watch him tremble.

Ellianna: I like to be reminded of what God has done through answered prayer and set reminders of His faithfulness. Outside my front door, I have a statue with rocks in a bowl. written different words that remind me of things or situations where God has answered prayer. Every time I enter my home, not only is it a conversation and witness piece it is also a daily reminder of God's goodness.

We encourage you to find ways, as a mother, wife and woman, single or married, to exhort others through the answered prayers in your life and find ways to display it around you, either at work and/or at home. Another way of keeping track of your prayers and the answers to them, which may be more private, is to have a prayer journal where each entry is dated. This keeps a track-record of answered prayers for both you personally and for your family. This is something we both practice and have found very encouraging in our personal lives as we look back and recount the Lord's answers to our prayers. Not only is it a huge faith builder but also a huge encouragement.

A powerful book we recommend in recounting the testimonies of answered prayer is the autobiography of a prayer giant written by Janet and Geoff Benge, titled *George Muller: The Guardian of Bristol's Orphans*. George Muller ran an orphanage for children in a poverty-stricken area of Bristol, England with little money. But he knew God had called him to care for the "least of these." Prayer was his main, and often, only resource. Reading this book will encourage your faith in the many ways God answered George Muller's prayers to provide for the orphans.

Going deeper in prayer and learning about this art of the language of God is an ongoing lifelong journey that starts with a love affair with Jesus. Without that premise, prayer means nothing and gets turned into a religious chore of vain repetitions. Sometimes God will just speak His love back to us in a simple, quiet whisper.

Ellianna: One time God showed me He loved me during a particularly difficult period in my life. I had recently finished college and was feeling pretty lonely. I regularly talked to the Lord about how I was feeling. One morning before work, I opened my front door to walk to my car and noticed that my sidewalk was covered in beautiful flower petals from a nearby flower bush. It felt like the Lord had blown these gorgeous petals along my path all the way to my car as if to tell me, "I love you. I'm taking care of you right where you are, and I am paving the way for your life with precious petals of my perfect love for you. I'm in control. I've got this and I've got you too." Sometimes prayers are answered in subtle ways we don't expect. I wanted God to do something about my loneliness, but He answered in a way that put my heart at rest, instead of giving an action plan. And that's okay, too.

The level of your friendship and relationship with God will affect what kind of things dictate your prayer life. In fact, we asked a very seasoned intercessor, our Aunt Mary Maude, if she could describe prayer in one word or in one sentence. She simply said, "Love." Without the love of God, we don't want to take up someone else's burden and bear it with them. We don't want to use our free time to pray for world issues or nations in danger. But the love of God for us, for others, and for this world compels us to fall on our knees on behalf of others.

To understand love on a deeper level, we have to understand the three types of loves: agape (divine love of God), eros (passionate love between lovers) and philos (love for family and friends). In the same way, to understand prayer on a deeper level, it's valuable for us as women, and keepers of the home, to understand the six basic types of prayer.

Praying in the Spirit: Speaking in tongues.

"And pray in the Spirit on all occasions with all kinds of prayers and requests. With this in mind, be alert and always keep on praying for all the Lord's people." (Eph 6:18 NIV) *"The Spirit searches all things, even the deep things of God."* (1 Corinthians 2:10 KJV)

Praying in the spirit, or using the gift of speaking in tongues, is a huge part of prayer. To some, this may be a new thing. If so, we pray you will take the time to search out this gift in prayer. If you have been taught it is no longer for the Church today, we'll just mention a few thoughts and Scriptures and let your own searching in the Word and listening to the Spirit of God lead you into all truth; as the word says He will do.

If God is the same today, yesterday and forever, (Heb. 13:8) then His character does not change just because we are not living in the "Old Testament" times. Jesus said He has not come to abolish the law (His word) but to fulfill it. (Matt 5:17) So, unless Jesus has come and fulfilled His word, like He did with the sacrificial system by becoming the only pure and perfect sacrifice, His word is not abolished but fulfilled. Likewise, the gifts of the Holy Spirit have not changed. That would be to go against the character of God. This verse of praying in the spirit is just as important today as it was when it was written. When we pray in the spirit, we know we are always praying the perfect will of the Lord because the Holy Spirit has searched the mind of God and is praying His will through us.

"In the same way, the Spirit helps us in our weakness. We do not know what we ought to pray for, but the Spirit himself intercedes for us through wordless groans. And He who searches our hearts knows the mind of the Spirit, because the Spirit intercedes for God's people in accordance with the will of God." (Romans 8:26-27 NIV)

2. Prayer of Thanksgiving: Giving thanks to God for what He has done.

We are commanded many times throughout Scripture to give thanks to God. Even when circumstances are difficult, we can always find something for which to give Him thanks. *"Give thanks to the LORD, for he is good. His love endures forever."* (Psalm 136:2 NIV)

Melissa: I had a story I want to share to help illustrate this point. But at the same time, I didn't want to because it is so emotional for me. However, my sister encouraged and pushed me to share, so here we go: I was diagnosed with multiple sclerosis in July 2017. It was a very emotional journey for me and I ended up spending five days in the hospital. I had a partial loss of eyesight in both eyes. This was my first experience with a hospital stay, and having to receive help and care from people in such a vulnerable and emotional time was a new and uncomfortable experience for me. The reason why it hit me so hard emotionally, apart from the physical challenges, is because healing is a passion of mine.

For some time, I traveled with a healing evangelist as one of his interns to serve the healing ministry of the Father to the physically afflicted and saw many miracles and answers to prayers. In my own life, as well, I have seen immediate healings take place, and I am always amazed at how God heals! The broken body of Jesus paid for our healing and I want to always grow in knowing His heart to heal me and others. I had to humble myself before the Lord and confess I didn't understand why this experience had happened in my life. I spoke with big words of faith but in my deepest heart, I had fears I didn't even know how to voice. I was ashamed and even scared to speak out. I cried a lot, and I didn't even know why. I didn't understand it all and just had to keep bringing my heart, my thoughts and questions to the Lord and trust Him no matter what my health or life looked like. We say we trust Him, but often we have to put those words to practice. I'm still learning how to do that, and it's a process.

By the end of my time, after high doses of steroids and intense treatment, I left with a fully regained vision. I could do nothing but give thanks and praise to the Lord as my Healer and good Father and for the prayers and support of friends and family. Tears welled up in my eyes as their love for me ministered to my spirit and soul. It's easier for me to serve than to be served. Perhaps the healing I needed wasn't of a physical nature but one of the heart.

One brother in the Lord even drove over an hour to come pray for me in the hospital. He himself had been in a wheelchair for many years due to multiple sclerosis and was under treatment at the Mayo Clinic in Minnesota (ranked #1 in America in 2018-2019 in U.S. News and World Report List for "Best Hospitals"). One night, at a prayer and healing service, the Lord supernaturally healed him. He came to the meeting wheeling in his wheelchair like always but left able to stand tall and walk with total and complete healing and use of his muscles and limbs. He still has the discharge papers from his doctor at the Mayo Clinic where it confirms his patient claimed to have been healed by God. His MRI test showed the evidence of this, and the doctor wrote he had no reason to doubt the claims of his patient. What a testimony! My healing was not the same as his. I did receive the healing of my eyesight back to 20-20 vision, however, and that was a miracle! All healing comes from Him no matter at what time or through what vehicle. All glory and gratitude to my Healing King and Lord.

3. Prayer of Praise and Worship: Praising God for who He is and His characteristics.

(Hebrews 13:15/Ephesians. 5:18-19, Psalm 96:2,9)

This prayer is not focused on what He has done for us, but on simply *who* He is. This kind of praise and worship is just about Him! It's lavish praise and adoration for who He is. The focus is on blessing Him and not about our needs and wants.

Depending on what your relationship with the Lord has been up until this point in your life will often dictate your prayer life and ability to enter into worship. It's easy to praise someone you know — harder to praise someone you don't.

For example, when someone is going through mourning or deep sorrow, they will often encounter and see the Lord in a new way: as a Comforter and Healer. Or if you experience a broken relationship or divorce, you tend to see the Father as a Bridegroom and Lover. Our experiences as women support our mold of how we relate, talk and worship Him, either as a Father or a Bridegroom. Ideally, He desires us to know Him as both. Because we women tend to be more in touch with their emotions, our propensity to worship God for who He is can sometimes come more readily.

While men worship the Lord, their format may tend to lend itself to a more masculine expression (which is needed), while a women's worship, often more expressive, tends to lend itself to a deeper feminine expression. When coupled with a man's expression of worship, it draws a more complete and beautiful picture of what worship was meant to be in its entirety. Both men and women are called to emulate both masculine and feminine worship — both attributes of God.

The beauty that a unified marriage gives the Earth is the chance to witness and behold the One that is being worshiped. To love the Lord with all your heart, all your soul and all your might is portrayed in a special way when it has the covenant bond of matrimony holding this three-stranded cord of love and worship together as one song to the Lord, giving it both masculine strength and feminine grace. A Godly wife and husband, in essence, are to love one another with a wholeheartedness even as the Lord says we are to love Him with all our heart, soul and mind. In doing so, this is a living act of worship.

4. Prayer of Repentance: Confession

Repentance is not just a one-time thing. It's actually an ongoing, a lifestyle and a process. Repentance means to change from walking in one direction to turning around and walking in the opposite direction, an about-face as it were. It's part of walking in humility before the Lord and being quick to change as we are transformed daily, and our minds are renewed. (Ps 51:1-3, Romans 12:1-2)

Growing up we heard our Dad and Grandfather say, "The most important words in any marriage (or relationship for that matter) is 'I'm sorry.'" It's so simple yet so hard. Apologize even when you don't feel like it. The same is true with us and the Lord; we should learn to repent and confess when we make mistakes. Saying "we're sorry" doesn't mean we're failing in our Christian walk, it simply means we're growing in maturity with the Lord and sensitivity to the Holy Spirit's conviction in our lives. Like Ruth Graham said, "A happy marriage is a union of two good forgivers." Learn to forgive but also to accept forgiveness. This starts with repentance and confession.

5. Prayer of Petition: Making requests known to God and asking Him to meet needs.

Even when we do make our needs and requests known to God, it is to be with thanksgiving, because He has already answered us and provided for our needs according to His riches in heaven. (Phil. 4:19)

"Do not be anxious about anything, but in every situation, by prayer and petition, with thanksgiving, present your requests to God." (Phil 4:6 NIV)

We can all recount examples when friends, boyfriends, spouses, family, etc. get onto us for not talking in the right tone. Think of Thanksgiving, in your prayers of petitions, as your tone in prayer. The Father is more likely to incline His ear to a petition prefaced with thanksgiving. He loves a cheerful giver. He also loves a thankful pray-er.

6. Prayer of Intercession: On behalf of someone or something.

Sacrifice is at the heart of intercession. Jesus is our great intercessor, and His dying on the cross was the greatest culmination of His life of intercession. Intercession is being willing to be a part of the answer to the very thing you are praying for. That is what Jesus did. He laid His own life down as the sacrifice that was needed. For example, sometimes in interceding for God to raise up laborers to go forth into the harvest, He may ask you to go and be the answer to that prayer. You have become part of the answer to the very thing you have prayed for. You have taken personal responsibility to see it come forth. All prayer is partnership with God and coming into alignment with His will, but intercession is probably the greatest example of that partnership.

"If my people, which are called by my name, shall humble themselves, and pray, and seek my face, and turn from their wicked ways; then will I hear from heaven, and will forgive their sin, and will heal their land." (2 Kings 7:14 KJV)

Regarding prayer in general, no matter what kind of prayer a person is using, it's important to remember that God hears us as the Apostle John reminded us, *"This is the confidence that we have in him, that, if we ask anything according to his will, he heareth us: And if we know that he hear us, whatsoever we ask, we know that we have the petitions that we desired of him."* (1 John 15:14-15 KJV)

Charles Spurgeon, a nineteenth-century evangelist, known as the "Prince of Preachers," said this of prayer: "I would rather teach one man [woman in our case!] to pray than ten men to preach." This famous preacher saw the value in prayer and recognized it as the core of a person's spiritual life. Praise God! We have living and past examples of people who know how to pray, but our best example is, of course, Jesus Christ.

"Christ, in the days of His flesh, when He had offered up prayers and supplications with strong crying and tears unto Him that was able to save Him from death and was heard in that He feared God."

(Hebrews 5:7 KJV)

Since childhood, we have heard Christians talk about the power of prayer and say things like: "We need to pray more" or "The problem with the church is that people don't pray more." We knew prayer was important, but we didn't know how to cultivate it in our own life. Feeling inadequate and incapable, we would just avoid prayer altogether, giving the enemy the upper hand he wanted because we believed his lies. Honestly, it was Satan's tactful lies that kept us off our knees. But something changed when we heard someone talk about prayer as a conversation with God. Suddenly, it became a lot more doable. Prayer doesn't need to be lengthy or long, it just needs to be a conversation, as conversations lead to intimacy.

A praying Christian is a dynamic one. Do you want to be a dynamic Christian, woman, or person? Then pray! Think of prayers as the currency of heaven. Our typical prayers of "God be with me today, bless me" are like us withdrawing $100 from our bank account for us to live on for the entire week when we have access to millions in our account. When we pray ineffectual prayers, we are withdrawing oh so little because we don't realize how much is available to us. Just like knowing the value of money and how much to withdraw for a purchase is important, it's also invaluable to know certain kinds of prayer and when and how to use them according to the transaction we are needing to make in the economy of Heaven.

The Psalmist urges us to "come before his presence with singing and thanksgiving." (Ps 100:2) When we start off our time with God in singing and thanksgiving, we find that prayers flow supernaturally. It can be as simple as thanking God for basic things like a roof over your head, a car to drive in, money for groceries and a family. These are things we take for granted every day because we are so westernized and have been given so much; it is easy to take advantage of them like we are entitled to them. But what if we turned our attitude into gratitude? We would have a lot less complaining. It's hard to complain when you're being grateful.

Sometimes when we pray, our prayers can be what we call "flare prayers." These are emergency prayers appropriate for certain situations. When we're having conversations in our heads and worrying about something, we will just speak out our worry and turn it into a prayer. This is a discipline. We don't always do this perfectly, but striving to do it is half the battle.

Prayer requires vulnerability. (Ps. 51:6) While it's important to understand and know different kinds of prayer, it's important to have a heart for God in our prayers. The best way to see this picture is to see the prayers of David who was a "man after God's own heart." (Acts 13:22) Friends are real and honest with each other. Some people feel (and we've fallen into this, too) that prayers have to be very grateful all the time and that you should never be grumpy or let God know what you are really feeling (as if he was really in the dark on that one). I'm sure we can all identify feeling hesitant about being honest with God, fearing that verbalizing negative feelings would somehow make us less of a Christian. But when we look at the Psalmist, we see he was honest with God, like we would be with a friend. As we invite God into our innermost thoughts and emotions, we become vulnerable and create intimacy, which is an invitation of in-to-me-see = intimacy. Having this kind of vulnerability moves your friendship with the Father from that of an acquaintance to a friend. To move into intercessory prayer, you must establish a friendship with God, not just be an acquaintance.

A good example of this is the picture of the relationship between a husband and his wife, which is the relationship God has with us. The Apostle Paul reminds us in Ephesians 5:23 that a husband is a picture of Christ and the wife a picture of the church.

Ellianna: There are times when I would cry on my husband's shoulders, especially when we were first married, and apologize profusely for my emotions and for whatever was bothering me at that time. My husband, Ben, would respond, "Honey, you don't need to apologize. I love that you feel comfortable enough to cry on me. It makes me feel like you need me and very close to you. I don't mind it at all. I like to feel needed." At that moment, I felt the Lord say to me, "And this is how I feel too when you cry to me." That was a big lightbulb moment for me. Take your worries to God and turn them into prayers. "Cast all your cares upon Him (God) for He cares about you." (1 Peter 5:7 NKJV) He wants us to cast our burdens on Him. Only perfect love does this. Remember, *"The Lord is near to those who have a broken heart and saves such as have a contrite spirit."* (Psalm 39:18 NJKV) David almost always ended his prayers of lament and raw emotion with praise at the end. (Exception Ps 88) Be raw, be emotional, but acknowledge God at the end of the prayer that He is God and we are not.

Chapter 5
Journaling: Recording Landmarks and Guideposts

"Set up road markers for yourself; make yourself guideposts; consider well the highway, the road by which you went. Return, O virgin Israel, return to these your cities." (Jeremiah 31:21 ESV)

The Jewish people were told to make "road markers" and "guideposts" on the road by which they traveled so that they might return to their cities where God had planted them. At the time this prophecy (Jeremiah 31:21) was written, the people of Israel had been held captive by the Babylonians for many years, and it was easy for them to forget their God and all he had taught them. Thus, they needed a reminder to help them remember who God was and all He had done for them. As we each are on our own "highway" of life, we too are to use scripture as our "guidepost," which He gives us as markers. Rhema is a Greek word meaning "word" but it's a concept God uses in scripture to speak a specific word from the Bible to us. We all can testify that the Lord has spoken a profound Scripture or "Rhema" verse to us, which can sometimes be during difficult seasons or trials or given on a daily basis. Those verses or Rhemas become building blocks on which we can build our faith. As we journal the things He shows us from His word, we are also able to go back and be reminded of these guiding posts, these markers in our life, of His leading and direction.

It's never too late to start a Journal. A journal is meant not just to recount the happenings of the day but also to express your thoughts and feelings based on seasons of life. As we write down our thoughts and feelings, or things God is showing us in His Word, not only are we, in a sense, "writing a letter to God" but we are also writing down things He's done for us; when we read them later, they remind us of His faithfulness.

How often have we gone back to our old journals and read the many verses God used to speak to our hearts during a different season of our lives. We have been reminded of ways God has spoken to us in prayers He has answered many years later. The future is a great place to be because you can look back and see the faithfulness of God. You can write things down that you felt God showed you in your time with him; you can write down ways God has answered your prayers. If you're a kinesthetic learner, the sensation of writing something down and engaging with a pen in your hand might be the best thing for you to retain what God has spoken to you.

If you've never journaled before, here are some good reminders to bear in mind. You don't have to journal every day. Journal when you're having your times with the Lord, and write down what He is showing you or what you're going through or feeling about life at the moment. Many turn their journal entries into prayers, ending with a request or petition, or praise of who God is. We both have gone through seasons when we journaled almost every day and then didn't journal for months at a time. Life can tend to get in the way, and journaling, for some, can be laborious. But what a joy to be in the future and read your old worries and be encouraged at how far you've matured or witnessed answers to prayers you've journaled.

> Melissa: "A strong memory from childhood was when a wise, elderly gentleman at church asked if I had a journal and if I ever wrote in it. He said, "You should always write in a journal because you think you will always remember things, but the truth is that you won't." Now that he was aged, he loved going back and reading the journals he'd kept in his life; it was as if he could relive his memories and life experiences that he would have utterly forgotten unless he'd journaled them. This is true not only in recording life memories and lessons, but in recording the things God has shown or taught us. I want to record His wisdom much more than my own thoughts about something.

Journaling helps verbalize what we're going through and helps us reason through things with God. (Isaiah 1:18) It helps us get to that place of seeing things from His perspective and not our own. Just reading the book of Psalms allows us to see this same pattern in the life of King David who wrote much of the Psalms.

"And the LORD answered me, and said, 'Write the vision, and make it plain upon tables, that he may run that readeth it. Do not forget the ancient landmark unless we forget God.'" (Habakkuk 2:2 KJV)

Let us take to heart Habakkuk's counsel. Journaling isn't just for yourself; it is also for posterity's sake, that those who read your life's account in the future can build on the lessons and wisdom you have learned. You can use journaling as a way to record your prayers as well as writing them down. You can also record the answers to those prayers in the same journal so it becomes an exciting, evolving story of your prayer life with God in a book form. As women, what greater legacy can we leave to future generations than our flowering of growth.

Chapter 6
Love is Time: Expressions of Love

"Do everything in love." (1 Corinthians 16:14 NIV)

Ellianna: When I was fifteen, sick in my parents' bed with a stomach bug and nothing to do, I remember seeing a DVD series titled "Keys to Loving Relationships" by Gary Smalley. I remember watching almost ten hours in one sitting of the nineteen-hour program. He talked about relationships with one series covering our "love languages." I was fascinated by this concept. Later, in college, I read the book *The Five Love Languages of God* by Gary Chapman. This also impacted me in a very profound way. The book explains that people tend to express and experience love in five different "love languages." The five love languages are:

- Acts of Service
- Words of Affirmation
- Physical Touch
- Quality Time
- Gifts

Reading and learning about this helped me so much because I always felt less of a Christian because I didn't have a need to spend time with God. I didn't need that to feel close to Him. I felt that is what a good Christian *should* do, but that wasn't me. After reading this book, however, I realized God enjoys *all* five love languages; after all, He created them. I'm sure there are many more He's created, but these help us finite humans understand the expressions of love in a very practical and real way.

I began incorporating these five expressions of love into my time with Him and not just my personal love language, which is Physical touch. I would make a conscious effort to spend time with Him and talk or listen, read His word, serve in ministry, give Him words of affirmation and praise Him for all He's done and the beautiful things He's created. I continued to worship and praise Him. Now I had a more rounded experience communicating to God in all of the five love languages.

The way we express love to others is often times how we'll express love to God. For example, if someone's love language is "Quality Time," they would feel most loved by friends, family and loved ones if they spend quality time together. In turn, people with this predominate love language will often spend ample amounts of time with God as a way of expressing their love to Him.

Someone whose love language is "Acts of Service" will show God their love by doing things for Him. We'll often see these types of people involved in ministry of some kind.

A "Gifts" person will often be very giving to God with their finances, time or other possessions that they could serve and love God with as a way to show their love to God.

There is also "Physical Touch," meaning people with this love language feel most loved when they have physical contact with others or are near them. And when you tell them you love them with a hug or your hand on theirs, it means the world to them. You will often see people with this love language expressing their love through worship, music and song. Because worship makes them feel physically close to God.

And last but not least, "Words of Affirmation" people tend to be very encouraging toward others and express their love to God by extolling His praises, writing books and songs. They use their words to affirm the character of God.

Know your love language and see if you can pinpoint how you relate to God in that way. Be aware of that and then try to incorporate loving God in the other areas you are not as natural in. It's just like having a spouse or friend — once you find out their love language, you try to express your love to them in a way that they receive love. Since God feels love in all the five love languages, we should try to express our love to Him through all of them. This is exactly what God did when He sent His Son, Jesus, in the form of a man to show us what love is in a way that we could receive it: the embodiment of God in Jesus. This is called the love of God incarnate, where God actually sent Jesus in the flesh to us. Our goal is to also be "love incarnate" to all those around us, to become a form of love that they understand and can receive. This is why knowing your love language and those of the people around you are so pivotal to showing the love of Christ. He knows how to relate to us in perfect love because He is so acquainted with each of us. We can be much more effective in reflecting the love of Christ when we understand the five love languages.

We must also learn to recognize God's love for us in the five "love languages" God has given to His Bride, the Church. These are reflected in the fivefold ministry mentioned in Ephesians 4:11-13 where God's love is expressed through the offices of apostles, prophets, evangelists, pastors and teachers: the fivefold ministry. Each function they walk in or give to the Church is different, but we must learn to love, appreciate and value each one. What gift or ministry has God given you for the Church? Are you a teacher? Do you have a shepherding or pastoral heart? Are you passionate about evangelism? In the same way God has created us uniquely with an individual love language, so too has God gifted us as Christians with special gifts to edify one another. In this, the word says His Church will grow up into the unity and maturity of the love of God.

Sometimes we can feel there is a block in our closeness to God or moments when we don't feel like we're communicating with Him. Whenever this happens, it's important to look at the picture given to humankind of what the perfect relationship looks like: Christ and the Church, exemplified in the marriage of a husband and wife.

We have seen that when a husband and wife don't communicate well, it can affect their marriage. The same is true with us and God: not relating to each other in a way that is relevant to the other person breeds hurtfulness and resentment, damaging the marriage. If I tell you I love you, but in a way that doesn't mean anything to you (a.k.a. not in your love language), then what I'm saying doesn't bear any weight. When couples get counseling on how to understand one another and live with each other in an understanding, respectful way (1 Peter 3:1, 7), breakthroughs in communication happen and marriages are rebuilt and become stronger. The same applies to our relationship with God. He understands us perfectly; after all, he made us. We, on the other hand, have to grow intentionally in how to relate to God in an understanding, respectful and honoring way.

Every person receives love in all five areas, but they typically are predominant in only one or two. Have a well-balanced relationship and express your love toward people and God in all areas, but know that He's crafted you with one special love language that He's designed for you to use to honor and glorify Him with. And when the body of Christ is loving God jointly in their unique love languages, God receives a well-rounded supply of love.

Spending time with someone you love is easy. When you first fall in love with God, it becomes such a joy to read the Bible and learn about Him and His ways. However, love is also a choice and not just an emotion. Sometimes we have to simply make ourselves read the Bible, even when we don't feel like reading. There is not a better way to get to know God as your friend than reading the very letter He wrote to you, His Holy Scriptures. In fact, throughout the Bible, God commanded us to do that very thing. A key verse on this is from the book of Joshua:

"This book of the law shall not depart out of thy mouth; but thou shalt meditate therein day and night, that thou mayest observe to do according to all that is written therein: for then thou shalt make thy way prosperous, and then thou shalt have good success." (Joshua 1:8 KJV)

God doesn't only want us to simply read the Bible, however, but to meditate on it *and do* it. We need to intentionally sit down to meditate on Scripture. But we can still be in conversation with the Lord about things we read in the Bible and ponder them in our heart as we go about our day. In Hebrew, the meaning of the word "meditate" is multifaceted depending on when it is used. Some of the meanings include: "to moan, growl, utter, muse, mutter, meditate, devise, plot, speak, imagine."

In essence, God wants us to not only be intentional about reading His word but also be creative and imaginative in living His word and becoming a 'living version' of His word. Since part of meditating is to mutter, or hum, moan… this has the connotation of singing the word back to God. Read the Scriptures out loud, but also sing them to the

Lord — especially from the Psalms — as they were originally written to be sung and the authors of the Psalms even gave musical notation with the different chapters. In memorizing Scripture, to get it deep in our hearts, it's a lot easier when we *sing* it, as a simple melody makes it easier to remember.

"Speak to one another with psalms, hymns and spiritual songs. Sing and make music in your heart to the Lord." (Ephesians 5:19 NIV)

Both of us grew up learning Scripture through songs, which we often come back to even in adulthood. Something about music and song makes it hard to forget. We challenge you, even right now before you continue reading, just open your Bible to a Psalm or favorite Scripture you love and begin singing it back to the Lord! He loves when we do this! And it doesn't only bless Him, it blesses you and others.

Chapter 7
Listening: The Fun and Scary Roller Coaster of Waiting

"But they that wait upon the Lord shall renew their strength; they shall mount up with wings as eagles; they shall run, and not be weary; and they shall walk and not faint." (Isaiah 40:31 KJV)

Since prayer is a fruit of our relationship with God and is a conversation with Him, we are not the only ones speaking. Friends speak and share things. That means there is a balance between sharing your heart with them and then listening to their heart as well. How boring is it to always listen and never get to share, or to always be the one speaking and never get a response or an ounce of feedback from the one listening to you? It's basically like it's a one-sided dialogue, which isn't dialogue at all. That would be a monologue or soliloquy. The very word dialogue itself means "conversation between two or more people."

Prayer is not just talking to God; it is about listening to Him too. It is a relationship that involves a two-way conversation. We can listen to God by being silent and waiting to hear in our spirit what His Spirit is speaking to us or by listening to what He is showing us in our regular Bible reading, but we can't limit God. He can literally speak to you through a photo, a person, a situation, or an experience. He even spoke once through a donkey and still speaks through visions and dreams or even through angels, as he did with men and women throughout the Bible (Mary, Joseph, Daniel, Joshua, John, etc.). Be open to how He communicates to you and always be listening. (Isaiah 19:11-12)

When God speaks to us, spirit to spirit, as He did with Adam, it's the most wonderful thing. Hearing from God makes us feel everything is right and in place. After all, He controls the universe. Sometimes when we feel we're not hearing Him well, or He isn't speaking to us, we know we just have to wait on Him and He'll speak. That's a promise.

A big part of listening is waiting. If we're always talking and never listening, how do we expect to hear from Him? Often times we don't hear an answer right away, but when we pray and lift something to Him, we know He will answer us in His good and perfect timing. That means we are to never leave the posture of waiting on Him. We can't just wait on Him to speak for ten minutes one morning and then leave that place of stillness and quietness thinking, "Well, I didn't hear anything in those ten minutes, so I guess He's not answering this one..." No, we've given Him time to answer, but His answering isn't dictated by our time table. He speaks when He chooses and how He chooses. Our lives belong to God, so that means all our time is actually His also. We must remain in that posture of being alert and vigilant for Him to speak through day and night. If, throughout the day, we're not vigilant about hearing His voice, we can miss His gentle nudges and reminders.

> Ellianna: I remember praying to God when I was dating before I got married and asking God to speak to me about directional wisdom regarding a relationship. I prayed for God to speak to me in a dream. I had a caution of being in a relationship with the person I was dating at the time and asked the Lord to guide me and lead me. "God, please reveal to me what my life would be like if I married this person." That night the Lord gave me a dream that revealed the person I was dating at the time cheating on me. As I prayed and asked God to speak through his word, He kept giving verses with the time period of 7 in them. I didn't know what it meant, but I felt in my spirit that God wanted me to wait 7 months before giving a reply to this man I was dating at the time to intentionally move the relationship toward the direction of marriage. As I communicated with this guy what the Lord had shared with me, we agreed to wait seven months before moving forward with our relationship. During that time, it was revealed that the guy I was dating was, in fact, involved intimately with another woman. As we navigate the trenches of life, we must hold fast to the counsel and word of God, and He will guide and direct us to the paths we should go. But we must listen for Him to speak to be guided.

Have you ever been in a situation where a Bible verse is recalled to memory that perfectly fits a situation or scenario you're facing? It's the Holy Spirit bringing that to mind to help us walk in the wisdom and guidance of the word of God. So, listening can be at a set time or throughout the day as we go our way. No matter when or how He speaks to you, be watchful and waiting, vigilant and expectant in your spirit at all times. This is a heart posture and attitude before Him that must be cultivated and protected. He doesn't show us things all at once; sometimes, it's in bits and pieces, spanning days, weeks, months or even years. This is when hearing God becomes that never-ending adventure and rollercoaster of expectant waiting. It can be so fun, depending on how you view rollercoasters, of course. Ultimately, waiting should be fun because it should drive us into the Lord's presence, which as we know: "in the presence of the Lord is fullness of Joy…" (Psalm 16:11)

A powerful verse in discovering God, hearing from Him and catching His secrets are found in (Proverbs 25:2) "It is the glory of God to conceal a thing: but the honor of kings is to search out a matter."

Being a king is an honor, but it's a lot of honor with a lot of responsibility and work. As children of God, we also have this honor of searching out the mysteries or concealed things of God; it's an honor but a responsibility we must humbly accept. This can be like God playing hide-and-seek with His children. It's as if He has hidden amazing things about Himself for us to find and discover if we'll play along and join the game with Him. He's a really fun dad *and loves* giving us that joy of discovering Him, but we have to choose whether or not to play along and search Him out.

"The secret things belong to the LORD our God, but the things revealed belong to us and to our children forever, that we may follow all the words of this law." (Deut. 28:29 NIV)

As we grow in relationship with God and become more and more mature, we begin to understand the importance of listening to Him. As humans, we have a natural desire to want to talk about ourselves. It's a conscious effort to learn the art of listening in any relationship. But as one grows in love, it becomes more and more natural to want to learn about the other person. This is where growth in your relationship with God comes from: your need and want of knowing Him and hearing from Him. As you grow and learn more about Him throughout your life, you'll find that you want to hear more about what He feels and thinks about things.

"The secret of the Lord is with them that fear Him, and He will show them His covenant." (Psalms 25:14 NASB)

As we grow in fellowship with God, He reveals to us his secrets, thoughts and feelings. Sometimes, He'll tell you things He'll do in the future. God will often speak to us through dreams if we but ask, wait, and listen.

"I will praise the Lord, who counsels me; even at night my heart instructs me." (Ps 16:7 NIV)

Chapter 8
Acts of Service - Intentional Love

"For whoever does the will of my Father in heaven is my brother and sister and mother." (Matthew 12:50 NIV)

Acts of service are something we often associate with action. In essence, it's love in action. Really, those who serve others are considered the greatest in the kingdom of heaven. (Matthew 10:26) They show their love through their actions. That must be why God says, "If you love me, feed my sheep," (John 21:17) because it involves an action. It could also be why God says, "Those who love me keep my commandments." (John 14:21) Again, action is involved in showing love. Love cannot be had without an action. Christ's death on the cross has revealed this truth to be evident. Throughout His relationship with His beloved ones, His love has been tested toward humankind with the continued rebellion and unfaithfulness of those who claim to love Him. Indeed, time has revealed this truth. The old adage rings true: "Actions speak louder than words." Jesus showed us His love in that while we were still sinners, Christ died for us — action. (Romans 5:8) Every act of service you do for God, whether living a godly life, keeping His commands, doing ministry etc., are all ways you show your love to Him, and it's also imperative in any healthy relationship.

Jesus makes it quite clear that to be his follower, we have to do the things His Father desires: the will of God. And at the heart of God's will is that we bring love wherever we are. The evidence of love? Justice. If there are people around you who are without food or clothing, do something about it! Through our acts, we show the love and justice of God. We do not earn His love by performance; because He gave up His own Son to justify us before His perfect holiness, we, in turn, have the same honor and call to lay down our lives for the Father. It's not easy to give up our rights for another, but that's exactly what Jesus did. He gave up all His rights to do the will of His Father, even when He chose to lay down His life on the cross.

"And going a little farther he fell on his face and prayed, saying, 'My Father, if it be possible, let this cup pass from me; nevertheless, not as I will, but as you will.'" (Matthew 26:9 KJV)

> Melissa: The Lord showed me this truth of laying down our rights in a profound way when someone gave up their right to attend a special meeting at a conference we both were attending. I really wanted to participate in this special meeting but hadn't gotten a ticket in time. Someone I hardly knew asked if I had a ticket and I answered, "No." Then, they responded, "I already planned to give my ticket to someone who didn't have a ticket because someone did that for me last year, and I was so blessed I wanted to do it for someone else this year." In the meeting, I was hit with the realization that this is exactly the only way any of us have a right or access to the Father, because Jesus Himself gave up His rights so that we might have the rights of sons and daughters! I had tears in my eyes as I was sitting down thinking of this and the selfless act that person had done for me. They proved their love in action.

We can do nothing less. Our acts prove who we are: sons and daughters of God, brothers and sisters of Jesus Himself. When we look at the way Jesus loved us and all the Earth, we're convicted that we do not love as He did by a long shot, but that is where He pulls us forward to look and act more and more like Him by laying down our rights one act, one day at a time. It is necessary to go before God daily to help us walk as Jesus did, and that's exactly how Jesus lived! He lived by going before His Father continually, and from that place, He was able to do and love the way the Father did. And as children of God, we are capable of doing the same thing.

Intentional love always exceeds a haphazard expression of radical passion. Would you rather have a man say he would go to the moon and back for you or a man who is actually *there* for you?

Melissa: Not all that glitters is gold. It's very easy for women who are more spiritually attuned to get drawn away by spiritual men who seem to play the part of Godliness but deny the power thereof. (2 Timothy

3:5) I was almost lured into an extramarital affair with a man I didn't know was already married. I met him at a national prayer and outreach event. We ministered together, and he asked for my number. After the event, he kept in touch with me with hours upon hours of phone calls. On our third phone call, he asked for my hand in marriage. Shocked, I said I'd pray about it. I was attracted to his spirituality and the power of the Holy Spirit at operation through him, which I had seen when we ministered together. As I was seeking the Lord's counsel and had asked for a dream, I received one the following night which cautioned me to not get involved with this man, either personally or in ministry. I reached out to a mutual friend and found out that our friend was actually already married. When I brought the information before him, he denied it at first but later came back and confessed and confirmed it. He said his marriage was in a rocky place. This man was acting in radical passion toward me but denying the true love he had vowed to his wife. Love always carries with it the fruit of actions. Love is just that: intentional. It's a byproduct of what we think in our heart not necessarily what we feel, for the heart is deceitfully wicked.

Good intentions without practice is false passion. Sometimes words fail to communicate the assurance we need. That's where actions really do speak louder than words. Talk can be undermined by lack of action. We can love God through acts of service that we do for Him. And He receives this as a sacrifice. Actions are the backbone of what we preach. Faith without action is dead.

"What good is it, my brothers, if someone says he has faith but does not have works? Can that faith save him? If a brother or sister is poorly clothed and lacking in daily food, and one of you says to them, 'Go in peace, be warmed and filled,' without giving them the things needed for the body, what good is that? So also, faith by itself, if it does not have works, is dead." (James 2:14-22 ESV)

Chapter 9
Meat and Potatoes of Fasting

"When you fast, do not look somber as the hypocrites do, for they disfigure their faces to show others they are fasting. Truly I tell you, they have received their reward in full. But when you fast, put oil on your head and wash your face, so that it will not be obvious to others that you are fasting, but only to your Father, who is unseen; and your Father, who sees what is done in secret, will reward you."
(Matthew 6:16-18 NIV)

During the time of writing this part of the book, it is the season of Lent. Lent is a time many Christians observe as a period (40 days before Easter) to draw closer to God and to pray and reflect like Christ did when he fasted and prayed for 40 days in the desert. Fasting is marked by abstaining from both food and festivities. But you may ask, "How does fasting help us draw closer to God?" Fasting, quite simply, is denying ourselves from something pleasurable so that we can rely on God for strength, honing our spiritual attentiveness and sharpness. That's why people will fast in certain situations because it draws them closer to God and God closer to them, thus, making prayers more keenly focused.

Two things happen when we fast which helps us become closer to God. First, we supplement our time of eating with time with God, reading the Bible, journaling, praying or however He leads us. We have time spent with Him that we wouldn't normally have and so we draw closer. Secondly, as we deny ourselves food, we find ourselves leaning more on God for strength as it takes great self-control not to eat food.

Historically, the meal time of the day, typically supper time, was considered a time of fellowship with family and friends. By omitting your time at the table with family during a meal time, your fellowship was now with a different audience. Obviously, a mom can't stop fellowshipping and cooking for her family while fasting, so it is a practice to grow into and adapt according to your own life circumstance and stage of life with children. The point is, by not eating food, you have more time to focus on your relationship with the Father.

Fasting can sometimes seem baffling or mystical. In fact, many religions besides Christianity observe fasting of some kind. Fasting works! There are many accounts of fasting, in Scripture and throughout history, the Lord has used to affect change. Since Jesus is our most perfect example, we always want to look straight at Him for how to fast correctly. Jesus fasted and prayed for forty days.

It has been observed that when Jesus said, "When you fast," in Matthew 6:16, not only was He putting emphasis and value on the discipline itself, but he also assumed the practice was already in place. And so, the "when you fast" statement was to guide them when they did fast. The act of humbling yourself in fasting is a good thing. Throughout Scripture, God tells us to humble ourselves before Him. In fact, God even has an opinion on the kind of fasting we should do:

"Is this the kind of fast that I have chosen, merely a day for a person to humble himself? Is it merely for bowing down one's head like a bulrush, for lying on sackcloth and ashes? Is this what you call a fast, an acceptable day to the LORD?" (Isa. 58:5 NSV)

God goes on to share what true fasting entails. It's not just abstaining from food but going out into the earth and actively being a catalyst of justice for the oppressed and needy. There's much to be discovered in this spiritual discipline, and however you feel led of the Lord to fast is how you should progress. Jesus himself was led "by the spirit" (Matthew 4:1) into His forty day fast. We too must be led by the Spirit of God in our fasting life.

Whether it's food or something else you give up in fasting, to pursue God and do His work, He will honor the heart in which you do it.

"So, whether you eat or drink or whatever you do, do it all for the glory of God." (1 Cor. 10:31 KJV)

If you want to go deeper in learning about fasting, we highly suggest, *Fasting* by Jentezen Franklin and *Atomic Power Through Prayer and Fasting* by Franklin Hall.

Melissa: I remember after I did my first twenty-one day fast, I was praying with my prayer group who met once a month (none of them knew I was fasting). One of the older men said to me, "You've been growing. I can tell a difference in your prayers." He didn't know what I was doing in private, but it was showing to the public. Fasting always brings out more of the character of Christ in us, and that is always on display no matter if we're praying with others or simply going about daily tasks. The practice of secret time and spiritual disciplines with the Lord always manifests in our personal transformation, and that is evidenced by all who meet us. Let God change your appetites for more of Him, and the world will become hungry for Him simply by being in your presence because you reflect His Glory.

While food is the typical thing associated with fasting, we can also include giving up certain things in our lives that take a lot of our time or that we find delight in, for example, a movie or TV fast, a social media fast, a dessert fast, a coffee fast, etc. When we do this, we are showing God we find more delight in Him than in all the other pleasures of life. When we abstain from something we enjoy and prioritize God, we show Him that He is the most important thing in our lives. A practical example that we can all relate to or at least understand would be a husband who gives up his football night with his buddies to take his wife out and just fully focuses on her and their relationship. By giving up what he delights in — to pursue her and focus on their relationship, he is showing her that he takes greater delight in her rather than in football. This is an occasional way to communicate that she is number one in his life. In the same way, we can do this with the Lord in areas that we find delight in. What can you give up to gain more time with Him and assure God that He is still number one in your life?

Ellianna: Once, for a fast, I decided to give up social media. I didn't realize how much I naturally gravitated toward social media without thinking about it. Because I wasn't visiting Instagram and Facebook during this time, I found myself reading more. I had more time to be reflective to focus my heart, mind, will and emotions on the things near and dear to God's heart. Thus, I became more aligned with God's will in my life and in my prayers.

Fasting is about drawing closer to God. We can do this through a myriad of ways depending on what we give up. When we remove distractions from our lives, distractions that are "time takers," we have more time to draw close to God and be available to listen to Him speak. Fasting is not just about the food you give up but also about the time and focus you give to the Lord.

Secret II - Personal

Chapter 10
Beauty: A Portrait of Christ (Adornment Within)

"Who can find a virtuous woman? For her price is far above rubies."
(Prov. 31:10 KJV)

One summer, in preparation for a girls' camp where we were speaking, we studied different gems and their value. We learned of one stone that could not be appraised because the experts literally could not estimate the cost because its value was too precious. Amazed, we realized a virtuous woman is too precious to put a price tag on, she's more treasured than the Earth's finest treasures. So, what is this kind of woman exactly? What is a virtuous woman anyway? Why is she compared to a ruby specifically? It has to do with the context a ruby had in ancient times.

A ruby was highly sought after and associated with wealth, wisdom, love and beauty, much like a diamond is today. When you think about how rubies were red stones, objects of desire, then it holds a whole new meaning. You could re-read the first part of the verse as: "Who can find a virtuous woman, for her price is far above wisdom, wealth, love and beauty. She is the object of desire, far more valuable than diamonds." Reading it like that makes it really come alive; you understand more fully what a virtuous woman's value was to someone who could find it or find her. If you had a ruby in your possession, in ancient times, you were considered very wealthy and full of wisdom. It would stand to reason, therefore, that a virtuous woman, if you could find her, would bring wisdom, wealth, beauty, love and passion into your life. To have a ruby in ancient times meant you automatically had all these things. The virtuous woman was indeed an asset, to say the least.

Virtue is not a word we use in our language today, so it's hard to fully understand its implications. To help us fully grasp what the definition of this virtuous woman means today, we also look at synonyms for the

English word virtue: goodness, righteous, moral, integrity, dignity, honor, decency, respectable, nobility, worthiness, purity, principles and ethics.

To go deeper still than the English synonyms for the word "virtue," let's delve into the Hebrew meaning for virtue, which is the word *chail*. It is a masculine noun that means "strength, might efficiency, wealth, army, force." In Strong's *Exhaustive Concordance*, the word "virtuous" is expounded on:

"probably a *force*, whether of men, means or other resources; an army, wealth, virtue, valor, strength, able, activity, army, band of men (soldiers), company, (great) forces, goods, host, might, power, riches, *strength*, strong, substance, train, valiant(-ly), war, worthy(-ily)."

The Hebrew word "chail" when applied to a "virtuous" woman, in this case, depicts her *strength*. That strength could include the strength of character, nobility, courage honor, determination, compassion, love, influence, etc. Also, kindness, purity, humility, integrity and resolve could be included, but this strength derives its *force* from the fear of the Lord.

These are all the things associated with being a woman of virtue. In essence, we could paraphrase Proverbs 31:10 to look like this: "Who can find a real virtuous woman? A woman who is all those female qualities but yet somehow has the same attributes of a soldier, a man of war, an entire army even! She is a mighty force to be reckoned with, one who is worthy, fit for war. She is capable and able, full of strength and valor. Yes, who can find a woman who has the same attributes as a male but lived out in a wonderfully, feminine way?"

This mesmerizing, bedazzling woman is none other than the virtuous woman. We like to call this beautiful example of a godly, virtuous woman Ms. Proverbs 31. In essence, a virtuous woman is a godly woman. She is made female, but she is one who walks out the character of Christ in her position as a wife, mother, homemaker, businesswoman, minister to the poor and those in her circle of influence, or whatever position she holds. Just as the character of Christ is the most beautiful, so is a woman who walks out that display of His perfect beauty in her own, unique, God-designed, female way!

If any of us compared ourselves to Christ, we would already know that we would fall short. If we compare ourselves to Ms. Proverbs 31, we would all fall short yet again. But Ms. Proverbs 31 doesn't compare herself to other virtuous women. She compares herself to Christ. He is fairer than ten thousand. (Song of Solomon 5:10) The rarity of such a woman is seen in the book of Ecclesiastes, also penned by King Solomon:

"While I was still searching but not finding — I found one upright man among a thousand, but not one upright woman among them all." (Ecclesiastes 7:28 NIV)

One opinion is that Proverbs 31 was written by King Solomon; however, others speculate it was the prophet Hezekiah, or another king of the time. Our opinion is, however, that it was King Solomon who penned the world-renowned chapter. If he, being the wisest man, could not himself find one righteous, upright, virtuous woman among a thousand, no wonder he is still looking for her when he wrote of her again in Proverbs 31. Who can find her? Solomon, or whoever the author was, questions again! Where is she? He wasn't lying when he said her price is far above rubies. He knew how rare this kind of woman was. How many of these virtuous women did he actually meet in his own life? It must not have been many. Desiring her manifestation, as he did, is the reason for this book you hold in your hands.

Will we, as a generation of women, rise up to this call of this portrait of fierce womanhood as portrayed in the character of Christ, wrapped in the title of Ms. Proverbs 31? It's not a call for the faint of heart, weak-willed or weak minded, but for the passionate pursuers of Christ and lovers of His glory being displayed and manifested in their lives and choices. We are that generation. We are the generation of righteous, virtuous women who answer the question "Who can find her?" with "Yes, find her in me!"

Some say the Proverbs 31 woman strives toward perfection, and to be like her is to be perfect. Yet we know no one is perfect but Christ (Romans 3:10). The call to be a virtuous woman is a call to be like Christ. We don't shrink back from trying to be like Christ because He was perfect; we let Him be our motivation, our aim, our goal (Matt. 5:48). Even though we will never be perfect like Jesus, we are made perfect because of Him. The same is true with the Proverbs 31 woman. Don't let the enemy deceive you into believing she's too unattainable and that it's not possible to be like her. The image of Ms. Proverbs 31 is not meant to discourage but to inspire. The enemy knows she's a force to be reckoned with. Strive to be like her. Let her be your inspiration and role model. You may fall short but strive to emulate your unique design and fulfillment after her. She's one of the many heroines of faith we can look to for inspiration and advice. Her beauty, in how she lives her life by priorities, is displayed in us as we reflect the beauty of Christ. Let's get it right by starting to live your life by priorities.

Chapter 11
Beauty: A Portrait of Christ (Outward Adornment)

"She makes coverings for herself; her clothing is fine linen and purple." (Prov. 31:22 NASB)

This amazing woman prioritizes inward beauty, but nevertheless, she gives attention to her outward beauty and adornment as well. She doesn't wear things without thought and intentionality. She is aware of her outward adornment. She gives time and attention to her physical apparel. She doesn't necessarily have to become a seamstress to fulfill this verse. She could easily just pay for the work of a seamstress (or store-made clothes) to accommodate her taste and needs, fit for the occasion as needed. It was the norm for women in Biblical times to make their own clothing. Nowadays, due to textile factories, it is often more economical for many to buy their own clothes instead of making them. She looks for good quality and complimentary colors becoming to her unique self, personal make-up and preferences. She knows what colors and styles enhance and compliment her physique, color palette and season. All this shows grace and honor.

Purple was an extremely rare and expensive color in Biblical times and throughout history. Purple was often associated with royalty or limited to those in the priestly service due to it being very expensive and difficult to make and manufacture. Even Queen Elizabeth I of England outlawed anyone to wear purple except close relatives or members of the royal family.

In fact, due to the cost of making purple clothing, it has been estimated that the Proverbs 31 women made at least fifty thousand dollars a year in today's salary, or considerably more than the average American living in one of the wealthiest nations in the world. The color purple still has a decadent, rich, royal flair to it even today. This woman had to do a lot of work to be able to wear such fine, lustrous, expensive clothing!

When a woman doesn't know that true beauty is from God, she will always be looking for outward beauty to make herself feel beautiful.

> Melissa: When I was a teenager and learning to put makeup on, I felt it was what I was supposed to do because I was growing into a woman. But, I will be honest, even though my body was changing, I still felt like an insecure child who was uncomfortable embracing the newfound beauty she was blossoming into. Putting on makeup was very emotional for me and it felt like I was trying to make myself more beautiful because I felt I wasn't pretty enough. It felt to me as if another verse in Proverbs was describing me:

"Like a gold ring in a pig's snout is a beautiful woman without discretion." (Proverbs 11:22 ESV)

I believed the lie from Satan that I was worthless and not deserving of beauty, that I shouldn't even attempt to improve what couldn't be fixed with jewelry, makeup or clothes that the world could provide. Satan is jealous of women's beauty and so, that is where he attacks. If he can make a woman hate herself and dress "manish" or like a slob, he is happy because hating yourself and how God made you is hating what the Creator made. If Satan can get us to hate what the Creator made, he is one step closer to defaming God and His creation. And if that strategy fails, he will try to make her worship her own beauty and put it on display to get others to worship her also. Satan tries these strategies because he doesn't want women reflecting the true, eternal beauty of Jesus, which is precious to God. In essence, it's actually an attack against God Himself, for God stripped Satan of his beauty when He cast Satan out of heaven. It was the worship God received in heaven that first made Satan want it for Himself and rebel against God.

Thankfully, as I began to grow as a daughter of God, I didn't cry when I put makeup on. I know the modern precedence of wearing makeup as a stigma for women is very much a Western, cultural thing and doesn't make or break true beauty. Sometimes I'll choose not to wear makeup to ensure I'm not getting my identity or self-worth and value from it. Most often, I do wear makeup. But if I feel the Lord wants me to take a break for a while, I will. As daughters, we submit all things to Him. Simple obedience to what He leads is what the Lord requires. Women of God, simply follow the leading of Holy Spirit in your own outward and inner beauty practices!

The Proverbs 31 woman is not ashamed to dress according to her identity, which is a member of a royal priesthood and daughter of the King. She clothes herself in graceful colors and feminine styles suitable for the occasion to steward and showcase her honored position before the King of Kings, highlighting her difference from rugged men and spotlighting her beauty as a woman. She does this in an air of honor and humility, not to flaunt or belittle her sacred worth. She understands modesty in both her attitude and attire, realizing her body is not her own but the temple of the Holy Spirit.

"Do you not know that your bodies are temples of the Holy Spirit, who is in you. Whom you have received from God? You are not your own." (1 Corinthians 6:19)

We once heard an interview of the English actor Iain Glen say that women who dress a little more covered up come across as sexier because it leaves something for the imagination. Our dress should point others to the beauty of Christ: modesty. When we dress to draw attention to our bodies, wearing skimpy clothes and flaunting our bodies, we draw the attention away from His glory and onto our own. Everything in moderation. Balance is one of the key factors to the Christian life — a tight rope that God guides us on. Our bodies are for our husbands to enjoy, not any wandering eye on the street. Show it the worth and value it deserves. Dress in a way that highlights your unique difference as a woman and creates mystery but leaves nothing to the imagination. Respect yourself in how you dress, and others will respect you too.

Chapter 12
Health & Fitness: More Than a Workout

"She girdeth her loins with strength, and strengtheneth her arms."

(Prov. 31:17 KJV)

This verse implies that the Proverbs 31 woman was able to do rigorous work. She was prepared because she was strong. Because of modern technology (we no longer have to make our own clothes and we have dishwashers), a woman isn't, by nature, going to be strong just by keeping up her home and preparing meals for her family. Therefore, to get the same strength that came about from normal living in Biblical times, we have to put forth a more conscious effort.

If you are so out of shape (and this could be due to being overweight or just lacking muscle) that you don't want to help out with something because it would be too physically exhausting, evaluate yourself. Is that what the Proverbs 31 modern-day woman would do? Gird yourself with strength and be ready. Make your arms strong either by the vigorous work you do or by working out, which can yield the same effect.

As sisters, we decided we wanted to join a fitness club and go together for accountability. Over the years, we have worked out in gyms and also done home workouts, but there is something about accountability that makes you get yourself out there and sweat. It's hard, and when we first started, whenever we would go, we'd tend to dread it. Yet, afterwards, we would always feel good. Now, we've become more accustomed to the routine and our bodies have gotten stronger and we look forward to sister time. The hour workout goes by faster now. Now we see changes in our bodies that motivate us. It's a sacrifice to get ourselves out of bed and go to the gym. There are so many other things we could be doing that feel like a better use of our time. But we've learned from a fitness coach that it's important to "find your *why* in health." Why do you work out? Why do you care about your health? We each have several different reasons. One "why" for both of us is to take care of our temple (organs, bones, muscles and ligaments) so we can be strong and healthy and be around for a long time to enjoy our families and be fit and healthy to do what God has called each of us to do.

An attitude of health is a very powerful tool a woman can put in her arsenal. If you master taking care of your body and making that a habit and discipline, every other area of life seems a lot easier to master because you've literally conquered and subjected your flesh. There is a very powerful spiritual analogy when it comes to health and fitness. What you sow is what you'll reap. What you sow in your life habits is what you'll reap. Two are better than one. It's not easy to do it alone. Find your why. Turn your excuses into your reasons. Find a partner and do something about your body. No one cares as much about your body as you will. So, start now!

In the culture Ms. Proverbs 31 was written in, women were no strangers to manual labor and hard work. She had to do a lot more strenuous work for her everyday existence and living. Today, however, most women are not doing hard labor for their livelihood. Training and disciplining one's body for optimum health and productivity is a basic principle of being a modern-day version of this ancient epitome of a godly woman.

"She sets about her work vigorously; her arms are strong for her tasks." (Proverbs 31:17 NIV)

What kind of work are you involved in? Are you doing your work vigorously and strengthening yourself to do it with excellence? These are the kind of questions we ask ourselves for the work set before us, and they are the questions all godly women should ask themselves to be the modern-day version of this ancient beauty. Don't go to the gym to try and sculpt yourself to perfection for the modern-day standards of beauty: sleek, skinny, stick-think, anorexic-model-physique. That is not the picture of ancient beauty. The Proverbs 31 woman was conscientious and mindful of her physical body and intended to make it operate at the best capacity, according to her specific needs and the work she was involved with. The Word says that the body is the temple of the Holy Spirit. This is also why this godly woman, in modern days, is zealous to be a keeper of her body. Just as a woman in love often desires to dress herself to please the man she is in a relationship with, so does a woman who has been born again by the Spirit, a follower of Jesus, desire to adorn herself with the clothing He loves, for He is her heavenly Bridegroom. The fruits of the spirit are things God Himself has given to us to clothe ourselves: "...Love, joy, peace, forbearance, kindness, goodness, faithfulness, gentleness, and self-control..." (Galatians 5:22-23) On this very topic, the Lord speaks to women specifically:

"But let your adorning be the hidden person of the heart with the imperishable beauty of a gentle and quiet spirit, which in God's sight is very precious." (1 Peter 3:4 EHV)

This portrait of beauty, God says, is precious to Him as it is a manifestation of the fruits of the Spirit in a woman. A woman could have a perfectly sculpted physical body but be anorexic in the fruit of the Spirit in her life, which is not healthy. The Word explains that a woman should be adorned with these qualities even while she seeks to enhance her outward beauty and appearance.

The woman who arises to the level of the Proverbs 31 woman wants what is precious in God's sight more than what the world calls precious and beautiful. How many women spend hours in the gym investing time and money into their physical beauty but neglect or spend little time investing in their spiritual beauty and cultivating the most important beauty of all: an intimate relationship with Christ that reflects His perfect beauty. Desire to reflect Him more than the modern version of female beauty. This ties in with a verse later in the Proverbs 31 chapter:

"Charm is deceitful, and beauty is vain, but a woman who fears the Lord is to be praised."

(Proverbs 3:30 ESV)

Our hope is that you work out to maintain health and keep up strength, but don't stress if you don't get your weekly workout routine in all the time. Working out can be seen as an act of worship to the Lord, obeying His words to treat the temple of the Holy Spirit with honor and respect.

By this He is honored and by this, He is worshiped. His health plan for each daughter is uniquely designed and planned by the One who perfects health and beauty. He gives each of us "beauty for ashes." As you go deeper into fellowship and relationship with the Lord, let Him search your heart as you peer into the mirror of His Holy Word. Cultivate a lifestyle of health that a strong body supports. But more than that, develop that strength of character and unfading beauty that is of the heart, the humble and grateful posture you hold before your Maker and Designer every day. Only by a right heart before Him can you give the right attention and focus to your physical body with the pure motive and desire to give Him (and those around you) your very best version of you — both outward and inward.

"Physical training is good, but training for godliness is much better, promising benefits in this life and the life to come." (I Timothy 4:8 NLT)

Chapter 13
Excel: Cultivating a Servant's Heart

"Many women have done excellently, but you surpass them all." (Prov. 31:29 ESV)

Have you ever known a woman who appears to have it all together? I don't mean all together like what Hollywood portrays as having it all together (i.e. material possessions, cars, big houses, maids, a happy life, best cosmetics, businesses, perfect body, etc.). No, I mean a woman who is truly graceful, managing her house, her body, her family, her business and giving to others. Not someone who appears to have it all on social media. But someone who *really* has it all? This ideal person does exist, she's called the Proverbs 31 woman. Yes, she truly did have it all. Many women do well, but the Proverbs 31 woman excelled above them all. Why? What made her different? She was above excellent. We believe her secret was in life balance, she knew how to prioritize her life. Let us say it again because it's so important: The key to being a Proverbs 31 woman and excelling above other women is life balance. She knew how to prioritize her life to live it out to its fullest.

The world is constantly pulling us in a hundred different directions, and it can feel overwhelming as to what to pay attention to at what time. Balance is the key to the Christian life, let alone the life of a woman.

How could someone manage everything that she did? She attended well to business, family, husband, and home, all while giving to the needy and poor. How does she do it? She's grounded. She allows others to help her when help is needed and she's able to live her life by priorities. If you don't get anything out of this book but that, it will be well worth it. You must allow time for yourself to organize your day and your thoughts so that you can be productive and rooted. When you find that sweet spot, then you will truly excel.

This verse drives home once again the rarity of true beauty, this dazzling Ms. Proverbs 31, a virtuous woman. Yes, many women can do excellently and surpass others in some endeavors, but the virtuous woman somehow ties together all these skill sets to build and hold her home and community together. She knows how to fit each task where it belongs, or place importance on each relationship according to its position in her life. She has a responsibility in her relationship with the merchants she trades with, but she also knows that her responsibility to her own husband and children surpasses in relation to the outside world. Her immediate place of domain is her own home; it is the womb of all relationships and over which she guards, protects and nourishes as carefully and intentionally as when she is a carrying life within her. This kind of woman, with her many unique gifts and talents, knows they are all tools for serving the very ones of whom she is a steward.

> Melissa: I was cleaning my family's kitchen one day, and with a family of ten, things can get pretty messy. My mom said to me, "Melissa, to be a wife and mother is to be a servant. You're constantly serving. If you don't know how to be a servant, you'll have a very hard time being either of those: a wife or a mother." Serving is a form of dying to yourself. You lay down your own agenda, plans or comfort to accommodate the needs (or sometimes preferences) of others, seeking to be a blessing more than to be blessed. Taking the form of a servant is how Jesus taught us to love one another when He knelt down to wash the dirty feet of his disciples. Another time, I had to clean our guest bathroom for some house guests coming over. I felt the Lord saying to me, "This is like washing the feet of My disciples, Melissa!" The bathroom is the dirtiest place to clean and wash, just like the feet were the dirtiest place of the disciples, having walked all day in the dirty, sandy climate of Jerusalem in their sandals. I don't always have the right attitude of a servant's heart in the menial tasks of everyday living, but the Lord helps me change my attitude when I think back to how the King of Kings came to the Earth "not to be served, but to serve." (Mark 10:45)

To excel and be a Proverbs 31 woman is to have the heart attitude of a servant. What is a servant's heart attitude? It's obeying the voice of the Master. A servant's heart isn't just doing things for other people and doing things for the sake of serving. It's knowing where you're called to serve and to whom. This goes back to your relationship with God and living your life by priorities. Otherwise, you'll get worn out and frazzled, trying to do everything for everyone. She knows where God is calling her to serve: to serve Him first, then her husband, children or family, household, in business and her community. We can't give you a cookie-cutter definition of what a Proverbs 31 woman looks like, but we can give you guiding lights of how she chooses to prioritize her life, knowing full well the Lord may call her to periods or seasons of time of varied focus or expression within those priorities (i.e. a nursing mother versus a single woman or empty nester). To excel as a Proverbs 31 woman is to be sensitive to the Lord in how He is asking you to focus on the priorities. He's placed before you in your current season of life. If you can cultivate the mindset of a servant's heart in obeying the voice of the Master, you'll learn the essence of a Proverbs 31 woman, and you will excel in all you do.

Chapter 14
Rewarded: Publicly Praised

"Give her of the fruit of her hands, and let her own works praise her at the gates."
(Prov 31:31 KJV)

What does being praised in the gates mean? The ancient gate in Biblical times was much like our current social media or news station; it's where all news could be heard, laws were declared, gossip was heard, business dealings were conducted, etc. Anyone who needed to know something about anything could go to the gates and get an ear full.

This verse is captivating. It not only shows that this woman has a reputation, but it is a positive one. She is known by her works and they garner her the praise of others. "Give her the fruit of her hands" applies to whatever she puts her hands to. Whether she is working with the merchants or serving in her household, tending to her family, the work of her hands pays off and gives her a return. It could be a financial return or the return of joy-filled, loving relationships where peace abounds. This kind of relational bliss is the kind of wealth money cannot buy. The fruit of her life is evidenced in her family and the world where she has an impact. Her world is a testament to the kind of woman she is. Give the woman the reward she has earned.

If you profit from something, reward yourself a little! If you find a way to save $100 a month, allow some ($15-$30) of that to go toward your "me fund." It's okay — it's Biblical. If you unexpectedly bring in $500 because of some business venture, allow yourself something you enjoy. Like the Bible says, "the worker [workwoman in this case] is worthy of his wages." (1 Timothy 5:18 NIV) Just because you're a mom doesn't mean you can't allow yourself some indulgences on occasion. It's called living a balanced life. Why is it so easy for moms to invest in their children or family but hard to invest in themselves? It's a beautiful picture of self-sacrifice, but the whole life of a mother is self-sacrifice, sometimes so much as to the point of burnout or exhaustion. Take care of yourself and, in turn, you'll take better care of your family. Pay attention to your mental, physical and spiritual health just like you do with your children. Now, we're not saying — become over indulgent or self-centered in taking care of yourself, but yet again, do all things in balance. There is a time and season for all things, even taking care of yourself. (Ecclesiastes 3:1)

We can hardly think of the verse for this chapter without remembering the beautiful example of its embodiment in our lives through our grandmother Virginia Bailey. "Grandmommy" Bailey was a woman full of life and joy. She loved bright, happy colors and was full of love for all of her twenty-two grandchildren. Her impact reached beyond her family and into her community and state. She not only was the president of Junior League of Little Rock but she was also heavily involved in beautifying Little Rock and everything that she touched. Her reputation proceeded her wherever she went. Because of her vision and initiative, Little Rock began to have flowers all around the city; it began to grow and prosper with new homes and real estate developments, which she initiated, that impacted the city's economy. She was a woman who used her gifts to change her surroundings. Even years after her death, people we don't know have come to us and said, "Oh, you're Virginia Bailey's granddaughter? I just loved her. She was such a lady and was always so kind and gracious to everyone!" One time, a furniture delivery man came to our family's house when we were moving. He realized we were connected to Mrs. Bailey and he went on and on about her. He said he remembered, as a mover, one time delivering some furniture for her. "Mrs. Bailey poured cold iced tea for us hard working men! She was just always so kind and nice to everybody." Years later, he was still remembering that small little act of kindness. Her works were still praising her. She also received many other honors and recognitions locally and nationally. Her works continue to praise her in the gates.

Secret III - Husband

Chapter 15
Trust: A Heart at Rest

*"The heart of her husband doth safely trust in her, so that he shall have no need of spoil." (*Prov 31:11 KJV)

Whether married or not, women have a responsibility to Jesus Christ, their Bridegroom and Husband. This section will outline practically how to live our lives with our husbands as a Proverbs 31 woman but also, as brides of Christ.

"For your Maker is your husband, the LORD of Hosts is his name; and your Redeemer is the Holy One of Israel; He is called the God of the whole earth." (Is 54:5 NKJV)

> Melissa: A woman I know from Mexico was left with three sons after her husband died. I'd met all three of her sons and saw something special in them that is not common for most young men in this generation. I knew their mother had to be someone extra special. When I did eventually get to meet her, I asked her how she dealt with all the pain of losing her husband. She said it was very hard, but she would not change it, because it was through that loss that she actually came to know God as her Husband and she would not trade that for anything. She clung to the Lord as her Bridegroom and Husband and let Him turn her mourning into dancing, giving her laughter for tears and beauty for ashes.

In the absence of a mate, the Lord encourages us to view Him as if He was our mate. Do we have decisions? Ask Him for guidance. Do we need provision? Ask for Him to provide. Do we need love? Ask Him to show His love. In fact, He wants to be our husbands regardless if we have an earthly one. Think about the things you would do with an earthly husband. You confide in him, share your heart with him, spend time together and listen to him. The Lord desires that same kind of relationship with us. He. Is. Our. Husband.

Our other grandmother, Gloria Spearman, is a prime example to us in this area. She has been a living example of someone who has made the Lord her first love, her Bridegroom and Husband. When our dad was eleven years old, she went through a divorce. Yet, through the hardship of that painful experience, she developed a personal relationship with the Lord and was introduced to the power of the Holy Spirit. Seven years later, her ex-husband, Jack, tragically passed away in a car accident. After all her children were grown and married, she remarried her second husband, Tom. They were happily married for almost fourteen years and then, sadly, he too passed away. Almost two decades later, the Lord blessed her with her third husband, Sam Spearman.

Through all these hardships, death of marriages and literal deaths, even losing one of her three children to illness, our grandmother has taught us that God is good, He is sovereign, and we can trust Him. She never forgot her first love. After all, God never leaves us or forsakes us. She was always grateful when the Lord brought her a companion, an earthly husband, because she saw him as a gift from the Lord. If we believe God works all things out together for good for those who love Him and are called according to His purposes (Rom. 8:28), then we can fully trust in His goodness. Our grandmother Gloria has taught us this. She was a strong woman, a hard worker. She was a single mom who raised three children, and she knew a thing or two about pressing on and leaning on the everlasting arms of God. She knew about the Comforter who was there for her in every trial and every pain of grief and loss.

At the time, our mother attended the same church as our grandmother. When our mother, Jo, asked the pastor for more understanding about the Holy Spirit, he directed her to our grandmother to learn more. Our grandmother Gloria essentially introduced our mom to the Holy Spirit with her son, Kevin, our dad there with her praying for her as well. In turn, our grandmother helped our parents to come together. Ironically, their relationship began because our grandmother strategically revealed the secret that our mom liked her son, Kevin. Although our mom was upset and a little embarrassed at the time that Gloria hadn't kept her secret, God used the information to help Kevin pursue our mom and a match was made in heaven. They have been married for 40 years and have eight children and several grandchildren.

Our family owes much to our grandmother Gloria. It was through her hardships in life that my dad saw her clinging to the Lord and was introduced to God the Father. Life will tear you apart; it can be rough. But as exemplified in our grandmother's life and countless women like her, God is the only One you can depend on to never change. He is the same today, yesterday and forever. Letting Him be your eternal Husband, going to Him when you have financial needs, emotional needs, and all needs, is the best place to start. And it begins by trusting God that He truly does work everything out for good, even hardships.

There is no authentic relationship without trust. Trust is the foundation for all healthy relationships. Think about a person you trust and why you trust them. Most likely, it's because you know they are responsible with what you give them, whether an item, a secret or a task. Because the Proverbs 31 woman looks well to the ways of her house and is responsible, because she uses money and is prudent and makes a profit, and because she is responsible with her husband, she is a safe place for him. He knows he can trust her with anything shared in confidence.

What does it mean when it says "he will have no need of spoil"? One of the meanings of spoil is gain. It comes from the language of the victor of a military exploit. The word is often used to describe the booty, spoil and abundance gained from victory. In essence, she brings her husband the elements of an abundant life. She elevates him in every sphere and element of his living. He can trust her to handle the set budget or task given, or responsibilities that he's entrusted to her.

Any general knows he is ultimately responsible for what happens to his army, but he safely trusts his lieutenants, captains and sergeants to execute his battle plans and the running of the day-to-day needs and necessities of a successful army. In the same way, a husband is the head of his home, but he safely trusts his wife to execute the home front as her domain. The Lord has set up this strategic battle plan for total victory in all society. Everyone knows that when the family suffers, all of society suffers. The breakdown of the home is the breakdown of society. Therefore, the virtuous woman takes very seriously her guarding of her post: the home. He trusts his wife to handle herself with dignity and honor around other men. He is not concerned she will use bad judgment. He safely trusts her. Ask your husband if he safely trusts you.

If not, ask him what it would take for you, as a couple, to get to that place of trust.

For those who are single, can the Lord trust in you? As a Christian, can your Bridegroom, our Lord Jesus, trust you to handle your finances and moral character according to His word? Are you using His principles laid out in Scripture? Are you living your life according to his word? Or are you doing what pleases you best and ignoring His will for your life? Can the Lord trust you to make wise decisions founded on his word? Can He trust you to act with dignity and decorum in business and socially as His daughter? Discuss with the Lord as you would with your own husband. The Lord desires to safely trust in us as His daughters as well.

Honor Jesus by being responsible with what He's given you. Let His heart safely trust in you so that when the time comes for an instrument to be used to advance His kingdom, you will be one of the instruments He uses. Does the heart of God safely trust in you that He will have no need of spoil?

A Word To Single Ladies

As single women, we have a special dimension in which to relate to God as our Husband. This truth is foundational to any woman, irrespective of whether she is single or married. In fact, it's the foundation for every child of God whether male or female. Letting God romance you as your eternal Husband is the foundation of the relationship with Him from the beginning. If you do not know His passionate pursuit of you as your Bridegroom King, it won't excite you to know He is coming back in His second coming for you, His Bride!

We can mirror our relationship with God in how to prepare for our husbands because one day, we will have to relate to a husband as our earthly head as we do with Christ. So, the best way for anyone who is single to prepare and get ready for a husband right now is to relate well to the Heavenly Husband, Jesus. Ask yourself, "How can I be a good wife to Jesus?" Desire to be someone the Lord can "safely trust." Just like the husband who has "no lack of gain," in what way can your heavenly Husband have no lack of gain in you? This question leads us to this verse:

"...An unmarried woman or virgin is concerned about the Lord's affairs: Her aim is to be devoted to the Lord in both body and spirit. But a married woman is concerned about the affairs of this world, how she can please her husband." (1 Corinthians 7:34)

There is a division of focus and attention from being a single woman to being a married woman. Division is not a bad thing when it is in keeping with the season and chapter you are in. When Jesus leads us into a relationship with the man He has for us, we can be assured it is a God-given distraction that He has blessed. When pursuing a relationship with a man the Lord does not have for us, it can be a bad distraction. I (Melissa) told the Lord I would rather be unmarried than be distracted with a man that is not of His choosing. I felt the Lord tell me if I wanted the one of His choosing and not my own, I would need to trust Him and wait.

This verse, for one, makes us treasure our years of singlehood all the more and desirous to use these years with the Lord well. Desire to be intentional with your love to our heavenly Husband now so that when the time comes, you can be intentional with your love to your earthly husband and eventually, Lord willing, your children.

We can love Him not only when we prepare for His return, but also when we prepare for the union with an earthly husband. Jesus left the Earth to prepare a place for us. Likewise, as we prepare ourselves for Him with the rest of His Bride, we prepare ourselves to be an earthly bride as well. That can look like learning cooking skills, organizational techniques, tending to our health, or even growing as a businesswoman to have streams of income to bless and support our families one day. The Lord will guide you to the skill to focus on.

In essence, love prepares in *the now* for the *then*. Prepare in the present for the one day coming of the Eternal Bridegroom and if single, your earthly bridegroom. In this way, we are hitting two birds with one stone. As much as the Lord can trust me now, in my single years, could easily be mirrored in how well my earthly husband will one day be able to trust me with the everyday affairs of our shared life together and running our home together. If you are single, be a pleasing and adoring wife right now to God and you will not disappoint the one He has for you later on. Again, any general will tell you as Benjamin Franklin so eloquently put it, "By failing to prepare, you are preparing to fail." Victory is in the preparation.

Desire to grow in Christ and your relationship with Him first. Develop a servant's heart like His. Prepare to one day walk out that relationship with Him with a husband and a family. Know that whatever investment of time or energy you put into your own relationship with the Lord will manifest in your husband's trusting you well with confidence.

Chapter 16
Intentional Love All Your Days - Prayer and Action

"She does him good and not evil all the days of her life." (Prov. 31:12 NKJV)

T here are two main ways we can do our husband good: in prayer and in action. One of the greatest ways to do our husband good all the days of our lives, even before we are married to him, is through prayer. The greatest way to love someone, and do them good, is to pray for them. You could even say it's a selfish thing to do because whatever investment you make in prayer is what your husband will receive down the road, and you yourself will be a beneficiary of those same prayers. Asking the Lord what and how to pray for your husband now, no matter if you've met him or not, are engaged or already married, is doing him good. Prayer works, and it's one of the things God commands us to do. Do your husband good now and lift him in prayer as the Lord leads you to pray. The book, *A Praying Wife* by Elizabeth George has really inspired us in this and we highly recommend it to any married or single woman.

Ellianna: As a young fifteen-year-old girl, I remember thinking to myself, "How can I do my husband good now? I haven't even met him." Then the Lord quietly spoke to me and said, "Your actions affect your reputation. How you behave now is how you can do him good all the days of your life." We often think that being good to our husbands only applies after marriage. But *all* our days not only includes the time from the early budding of youthful marriage to the fading into old age together, but it also means all the days before we are married. This can be lived out when you're single by living a principled life. I remember telling my now husband when he asked to kiss me on our second date that, "I was saving that for someone special." I later told him that I wanted my first kiss to be to the man I felt like I was going to marry. It was hard remaining pure while dating, but having standards and safeguards really helped me when I was dating pushy guys. I wasn't perfect all the time; I definitely could have done better, but in the area of purity, I thank God because he kept me a virgin before I got married, and I was able to give that gift of virginity to my husband, which is something he greatly cherishes.

If you are not a virgin, you can still give your husband and the Lord, the heart of a virgin now by choosing to live a life of physical purity, becoming a committed virgin from this day forward, remaining sexually abstinent till the right time. God already forgot all of our sins because of the blood of Jesus. No sin is bigger than the perfect sacrifice of God's own Son. We all have had sins we struggled moving past, not believing we are forgiven, but the truth is we have been forgiven once we have given our lives to Christ and confessed Him as Lord. Nothing can change that. God does not judge us, and neither can we judge one another. God put His judgment of sin on His Son. Jesus took God's wrath and judgment on sin for us, making us pure and spotless under His blood. Offer your body as a living sacrifice to God and commit in your heart to abstain from sex until marriage and watch God redeem what was once lost. He gives us beauty out of ashes, redemption from sin.

Our mom felt our dad would be her husband and prayed for him for two years before they ever went on a date. Her sister, our aunt, also had a similar kind of experience. She also felt the Lord highlighting a specific man to her to pray for. She didn't know if he was the one the Lord had for her, but she knew he would be blessed through her prayers regardless of whether he was to be her husband or not. Sure enough, similar to our own mother's experience, the Lord brought them together and they are now happily married.

Melissa: I had a somewhat similar experience when I really liked a guy in college. I decided to just start praying for him and whether or not he was one the Lord had for me, he would get a lot of blessings through my prayers! We never dated or got into a relationship, but I began to see changes in him that correlated with exactly the things I was praying for him. One thing I prayed was that he would receive more joy because I noticed he often had a downcast or somber air about him. At the end of one of our semesters, he said he felt the semester had been all about

God showing Him how to get joy in Him and how much joy he felt! You can only imagine the joy in my heart in hearing him share this! So, know this… whatever prayers you're praying or blessing your husband with, they are doing him good now, even if you don't know him yet. A good safeguard in praying for someone you like is to pray for them and for your husband generically. Even if the guy you like isn't the one you are to marry, your husband will be blessed too.

In addition to our reputation, based on our actions, and prayers, another way to do your husband good before you meet him is by being business-minded. If you save up money before getting married and bring that into the marriage, then you're doing him good all the days of your life. If you start a business before getting married and continue that into marriage, you're doing good all the days of your life.

Think about what you can do now to bring honor to your husband when you're married. Remember that the Proverbs 31 woman is virtuous. She's very valued and full of wisdom. She's sought after. How can you be that woman now? In purity, yes! In finances, yes! In business, yes! In prayer, yes! In reputation and actions, yes! Your actions make up your reputation so what can you do now to be a blessing? Perhaps the best thing beyond the practical ways of doing good is to have a solid relationship with God. As you are on solid ground, so will your husband be. You are the other half of your marriage relationship now. The husband is the water, but you are the current. You influence where and how the water moves. So, make sure your influence is one of strength, honor and integrity. In hard times, let your kind and faith-filled words encourage your husband. Don't foster words filled with fear and anxiety because you are fearful of what lies ahead. Be a solid rock in the word of God. Express your fears and concerns to Him first. Then, when you express concerns or fear to your husband, you'll be better positioned to be a woman of virtue, ready to give wisdom. This is how you can do good to your husband all your days!

Chapter 17
Concerned with His Reputation

"Her husband is known in the gates, when he sits among the elders of the land."
(Prov 31:23 NKJV)

As children, our parents have always told us how we behaved was a reflection on them. Especially when we would dine out or be in formal situations, they would always remind us of dining manners and rules of how to behave in public. If our actions are an indication of our character as a child, wouldn't the same be true as adults? As Christians, our actions, what we choose to watch, what we choose to listen to, what we fill our minds with, what we choose to stand up for and talk about on social media or in person, are all reflections of Jesus Christ in us. If we choose to tell friends we can't make a movie (knowing it wouldn't be honoring the name of Christ), and later someone asks about why we didn't go, doesn't that action reflect well on the name of Christ? The same is true with children. When children behave well in public and have good manners and are kind and helpful to others, that reflects well on their parents. They then become "known" as good parents because of their children's behavior. Just as children represent their physical parents, so do we, children of God, represent our Father in Heaven and we are "known by our doings" and by our character. Actions speak louder than words.

"Even a child is known by his doings, whether his work be pure, and whether it be right." (Prov. 20:11 KJV)

The words of the Apostle James in the New Testament illustrate this beautifully:

"What does it profit, my brethren, if someone says he has faith but does not have works? Can faith save him? If a brother or sister is naked and destitute of daily food, and one of you says to them, 'Depart in peace, be warmed and filled,' but you do not give them the things which are needed for the body, what does it profit? Thus, also faith by itself, if it does not have works, is dead. But someone will say, 'You have faith, and I have works.' Show me your faith without your works, and I will show you my faith by my works. You believe that there is one God. You do well. Even the demons believe — and tremble! But do you want to know, O foolish man, that faith without works is dead?

Was not Abraham our father justified by works when he offered Isaac his son on the altar? Do you see that faith was working together with his works, and by works faith was made perfect?" And the Scripture was fulfilled, which says, "Abraham believed God, and it was accounted to him for righteousness." And he was called the friend of God. You see then that a man is justified by works, and not by faith only. Likewise, was not Rahab the harlot also justified by works when she received the messengers and sent them out another way? For as the body without the spirit is dead, so faith without works is dead also." (James 2:14-26 NKJV)

We learn here that what we do reflects on those in our lives. As a mother, as a wife, as a woman, as a person, as a citizen, everything we do reflects on those we hold dearest to us. The same is true with the virtuous woman because she is a woman who is known, a woman who has complete management of household affairs. This frees up time for her husband and gives him full leisure to devote himself to the civil interests of the community. Therefore, he is known by her well-management of the home, how she provides and clothes him; by her reputation, he is known. Just like a child is to a parent or a Christian is to Christ, or faith and actions, so is a wife to her husband.

It's not just actions alone, but also our words. If I'm speaking negatively about my husband to my girlfriends, am I making him known? Yes, but in a bad way. Not only is it rude to speak negatively about your husband in front of others, but it is also not having the law of kindness and gentleness on your lips. It's not kind. So, stop doing it. What are you really accomplishing by airing out his dirty laundry? If you are having marriage problems, pick a few trusted women you admire to be your confidant and to help you navigate through marriage struggles, but stop tearing down your husband's reputation. He will be known for the wrong reasons. One exception to this is if your husband is sinning against you or hurting you or your children in any way. Then, of course, you have a responsibility to get help and get out of that dangerous situation as soon as possible. There is no justification for violence in marriage. This is a situation where being concerned about your husband's reputation would not apply because of his sin toward you.

As little girls, our mother taught us how to interact with men and how to honor them. She did an excellent job in that area, not only by living out an exemplified life but also by sharing sayings and stories. One story she shared was about her mother. Our grandmother was a real estate developer, very well known in Little Rock as a gracious and ladylike businesswoman, which is a very rare combination in today's culture. Our mother told the story of how our grandmother, whenever she was president on a business or executive board, would make our grandfather vice-president. Or, if she started a board, she would make him president, and in doing so, he became known and respected as her confidant. She always spoke tenderly and kindly to him. The years following my grandmother's death, many people would comment on what a lady our grandmother was. Wait, you can be a lady in business? But culture teaches us you have to be strong and tough, right? No, that's just what the feminist movement feeds you because in doing so, you tear down men and their masculinity and the God-given roles they were meant to fulfill.

Ellianna: Out of five girls in the family, I was the only tomboy. This could be because I had two older brothers right above me, but my mother handled me well. She always told me, "Ellianna, you can do anything a boy can do, as long as you do it in a ladylike way." Because I loved to climb trees with my brothers, my dress would always fall over my face as I climbed, leaving me exposed to indecencies. So, I quickly learned that if I wanted to keep up with my two older brothers I would either have to change clothes or figure out a way to climb a tree in a dress gracefully. I learned both. But the main thing I learned is I'm not inferior or less than men, no, I can do anything a man can do, as long as I understand my unique position as a woman and behave like a lady. This was easy for me because I had my grandmother and mother as examples of Christian businesswomen and virtuous women. In summary, our actions and our attitude reflect on our husband's reputation.

Merriam-Webster Dictionary defined attitude as: "a position assumed for a specific purpose, a mental position with regard to a fact or state, a feeling or emotion toward a fact or state." Our thoughts affect what we say, which in turn affect our behavior. If we want to challenge ourselves to make our husband known in the gates, we have to go back to our attitude toward him. If we are known by our actions then surely, we must return to our words, for by them we are held accountable and judged for either good or evil. (Matthew 12:37) Nothing holds more power than our tongues. Life and death, blessing and cursing are in them. It can be very easy to believe because you don't have a husband, you don't need to worry about what you say. But whether married or single, you can still bring honor or disrespect to the men in your lives by what you say about men, in general, when you are among close friends, or if married, what you say about your husband. Although this verse is specifically talking to women who are married, we believe this relationship principle can also apply in our attitude toward men in general.

The verse for this section insinuates that because of his wife, the Proverbs 31 woman's husband is known among those in high power (the elders of the land). He is elevated in part because of the actions and words spoken by his wife. What a woman says and does is a reflection on her husband/boyfriend/fiancé, etc. Be a crown to your husband, make him look better and empower him. How many times have we heard stories of wives who say one thing to their friends only for their husbands to find out later what they said about them and feel ashamed? Let your attitude toward the man God has placed in your life be one of not only love, but of honor and respect. The Hebrew word for honor (kabad or kabed) simply means heavy or weighty. The idea of honor here simply means that we can honor our husbands by simply having their words carry weight with us. We pay attention when they give advice and their words carry more honor from us than any other person.

n this same way, a single woman can foster this same attitude of honor in regard to the Lord, as He is her husband, being more concerned for His reputation. She is to be concerned with God's reputation first before that of a boss, employee, co-worker, or business partner. In essence, every relationship she has, she carries with the attitude of honor, both toward men and women. She is concerned to honor and build up all she is connected to. In this way, she is making the Lord's reputation known in the gates of the marketplace, even as a married woman does for her husband in all her interactions with others. How we honor the Lord is shown in how we honor those around us.

Chapter 18
Get Your Finances Together, Together

"She is clothed with strength and dignity, and she laughs without fear of the future." (Prov 31:25 NLT)

Financial health starts with a disciplined mind. When we view finances according to the principles of God's word, we can then have rest and peace. Often when people think of finances, they think of budgeting and balance sheets. You can't create a budget, however, without looking to the future. A Proverbs 31 woman, whether married or not, does look at the future and plans accordingly to these very principles: giving generously, tithing and avoiding debt, to name a few. All of us can easily be overcome with fear if we let our minds go their own way and do not choose to do what the Word says, taking every thought captive and bringing it into subjection of Jesus Christ. (2 Cor. 10:5)

As women, we often have the tendency to be given to worry when we think of the future, perhaps especially in finances. But that is not the high calling of a daughter of Christ or the Proverbs 31 woman we are called to be. To be clothed with dignity and honor, we must have the mindset of a warrior. We laugh at the future or the unknown because we know who our God is and that He is holding our future together. We have to actively train our minds and choose to obey the word of God as He tells us:

"Do not conform to the pattern of this world, but be transformed by the renewing of your mind. Then you will be able to test and approve what God's will is—his good, pleasing and perfect will." (Romans 12:2, NIV)

The Hebrew word "ezer," used to describe women from Genesis 2 and most often translated "helpmate," is often translated as "warrior" and used to describe God Almighty elsewhere in the Old Testament. One could argue the very essence of being a woman is to be a warrior for God. How incredible is that?

We once heard another Hebrew scholar break down the word "helpmate" as something meaning an equal counterpart. The picture being that of a man and woman standing face to face as equals and suitably matched partners for the joint work assigned to them from God. Eve herself helped her husband, Adam, with his work of tending to the Garden of Eden that the Lord had placed before him. In essence, a wife as a helpmate is one who is equally matched with her man, and their work is a joint effort together as a team.

This affirms that we must feed on the word of God daily and eat of the bread of life! We've all been through times where we've given way to fear. Whenever fear wants to creep in and rip your strength and dignity away, fight back with quoting scripture. After all, God's word is likened to a sword. Use it as a weapon whenever the enemy taunts you with fearful or degrading thoughts. We've all been tempted with thoughts of fear, such as: "You'll never lose weight," "You're not pretty," "You won't ever get out of debt," "Your children will grow up corrupt," "You won't ever succeed at this." But where do these thoughts come from? Not from heaven, that's for sure. The next time you're tempted with fearful or disparaging thoughts, take out your sword of truth, God's word, and use it against those thoughts. (Ephesians 1:18)

It's the *Word* of God that reminds us who we are and helps us keep our eyes and focus on what is the glorious inheritance that is ours as His daughter. It is not one of fear or self-doubt, but of victory and a conquering spirit. Jesus speaks of such ones as an overcomer! When discouraged about finances, let faith rule the day, not fear. Face your faith, not your fear.

When you exercise being an overcomer, you are conquering finances and refusing to be a slave to fear. Because the Proverbs 31 woman is a believer in the King of Kings and knows her Lord, she knows that He is our Overcomer! He has overcome sin and death and that same spirit that resurrected Him is alive in her! *"...for everyone born of God overcomes the world."* (1 John 5:4,5)

Wow, isn't that incredible? This righteous Proverbs 31 woman may not be perfect, but she is daily being transformed by the word of God; she is going from victory to victory, from glory to glory. Her perfection is being cultivated and coming forth as pure gold. The word says the righteous person falls seven times but gets back up and keeps going. (Proverbs 24:16) In the same way, a Proverbs 31 woman, whenever she fails in finances, learns from those mistakes and becomes wiser and stronger, not weakened and bitter.

She clothes herself with strength and dignity, with the word of God guarding her thoughts and ways of thinking. She is adorned with the armor of a warrior, so even when (not if but when) she falls down, she doesn't stay down but gets back up again and keeps going with the joy promised to her as an overcomer.

> Ellianna: A few days before I got married, my dad took me out to lunch and handwrote a list of things he thought made up a successful marriage. One of his bullet points was: "Get your finances together, together." As we moved into married life, my husband and I tried to do that — to a certain extent. My husband would write a proposed budget and then we reviewed it together. But after a year and a half of marriage, we had to pay thousands of dollars to repair our car. We had the money, but it set us back on paying off some debt we had. I'm so goal-oriented that this unexpected expense threw me for a tizzy. We both were stressed, perhaps me more than him. I didn't feel like my car was falling apart, I felt like my life was falling apart. In the middle of all this chaos, as I was driving home, looking out the window, I thought of the phrase, "She laughs without fear of the future." How does a woman look into the face of future without fear? How can you hold yourself high with strength and dignity when you're drowning in bills, debt, illness and/or uncertainty or even a broken heart? One week before all this happened, we decided to take a Dave Ramsey course to learn how to better manage our finances. We were actually doing really well when we signed up for the class, or so we thought. We'd had more in our savings, were making aggressive dents in debt, and then, life happened. I later joked to my husband that maybe the Lord gave us a lot of unexpected bills before the class started so we'd become familiar with a feeling we'd never want to feel again. After getting on the same page, taking the financial peace

workshop, and coming up with a plan, we both felt confident that when something unexpected happens again, we'll be able to hold our heads high with confidence, strength and dignity, because we now had a plan. As God reminded his people, "Without a plan/vision, my people perish." (Prov. 29:18) And in so doing, we look well to the ways of our household and store up for anything unexpected that may happen. This is the practical side, and I think it's important. And wouldn't you know it, no sooner had we paid off our car repair, another unexpected expense came our way! While writing this book, my husband, Ben, was up for hours one night with a severe toothache. The next morning, we learned that it was symptoms of a root canal infection. Again, another expensive unexpected bill. But this time, my response was different. I could truly look at the future and laugh, knowing that God would provide all our needs. And indeed, He did. He provided the money we needed right before my husband came out of the doctor's office by money deposited into our account from investments we had made, which amply covered the bill. We had the money in our businesses to pay for it, but I felt strongly that God wanted us to grow our businesses debt-free. And, so far, we've done that. I prayed in the dental office as my husband was getting his teeth worked on, "Lord, if you want me to not go in debt in my business and just keep investing what I earn back into my company, then you've got to come up with a different solution of how to pay this bill." And, sure enough, He did. God's good like that.

The other side of having a plan is having a heart at rest. God gives us His principles of how to have a heart at rest and for getting financial peace found in His word.

"You keep him in perfect peace whose mind is stayed on you, because he trusts in you." (Isaiah 26:3 ESV)

While the heart at rest is important, it's a two-sided coin. One side of the coin is us trusting God as our Provider, and the other side is us being wise stewards of what He's given us to manage. These financial principles are uniquely laid out in Dave Ramsey's book *The Total Money Makeover*. Finances are a real concern for many people. Don't keep living in stress; manage your life and finances the way God instructed, and you will have a heart at rest as a result. You will be able to look at the future and laugh at the face of whatever it throws at you. Take time for yourself to be alone, to be quiet, to get grounded and reflect and meditate on life. Not wanting to be in a financial harassment situation again or disparaging in your own self-degrading thoughts can be a huge motivator for us to get out of debt and into financial peace. But it all starts at the feet of Jesus and keeping your mind fixed on Him and His Word. God has given us a weapon: His Word. Now, we have to learn how to use it to ward off Satan and his evil hosts. No one has time for unnecessary stress. Get your finances together, together.

Chapter 19
Lead by Example: Couple Time

"Her children arise up, and call her blessed; her husband also, and he praiseth her." (Prov. 31:28 KJV)

A s children, we always looked forward to Friday nights. It was a time when our parents would leave the house for "couple time" or "date night," which meant we children would go to the movie store (yes, we just dated ourselves) and rent a VHS movie(s) and order pizza and have friends over. For us, it was "fun night." The important lesson wasn't just the fact that our mother made time for date night; the deeper lesson we learned was that dad came first before the children. Our mother never told us this point blank, but we all knew this.

Leading by example doesn't mean you're perfect, as our mother was not. But even in her imperfections, she led by example in showing us how to apologize, how to forgive, how to say "I'm sorry," how to humble herself before her husband and admit when she was wrong. We were all watching and thought this behavior was normal. We saw our father also walking in this same manner toward her and was always quick to apologize to our mother or even to us when prompted by the Holy Spirit to do so. As we matured into adulthood and ventured into dating and the real world, we quickly realized this was not as easy as they made it look. However, the example set by our parents was like graceful jewels that we wore around our necks. Everywhere we went, people commented on the behavior and kindness of our mother's children. As a wife, a mother, a woman, led by example, let your mistakes be occasions to teach and be a lesson of humility.

"In the same way, you wives, be submissive to your own husbands so that even if any of them are disobedient to the word, they may be won without a word by the behavior of their wives." (1 Peter 3:1 NASB)

Even husbands arise and call their wives blessed because she can lead her husband by simply her behavior and what she does instead of what she says. Again, we saw our mother do this with our dad repeatedly. There were times he would make decisions our mother did not feel good about, but through her behavior, he was led to find answers in Scripture. There were times, engraved in our memories, when we were younger, and our dad would apologize in front of the whole family for how he had spoken to our mother. Both our parents showed humility and honor toward each other, and as children, this taught us an invaluable lesson that people we admire make mistakes too. The true character of a person is revealed by how they respond when they make mistakes, responding to them honestly instead of trying to hide them. In this way, our father rose up and called our mother blessed, because she had led by example, not demanding her own way, but simply by her actions and behavior.

Her husband is known in the gates. Remember, the gates were the place where the "elders" or the "leaders" would meet and discuss things, making decisions that affected the city and those in their realm of influence. Basically, her husband has a voice in his place of influence that impacts and brings change to those he affects. He obviously holds honor with his colleagues or coworkers because he is known in a place where honored men frequented; he was listened to. If a man is respected at home by his wife, and she supports him in using his leadership for positive impact, then her husband will surely be known in the gates and walk in that same degree and honor that she fosters at home. People often mirror their home life in public or in the marketplace at work. She cultivates honor and he walks in that honor with his community. As a wife, you have the power to set him up for success in how you honor and treat him at home.

"An excellent wife is the crown of her husband, but she who brings shame is like rottenness in his bones."

(Proverbs 12:24 ESV)

She does not cause him shame by her behavior or treatment of him, even in private. If she did, this "rottenness of bones" would most assuredly affect any kind of leadership he walked in outside of the home, negatively affecting his work and his social life. No, she crowns him with splendor and honor, making him the king in their home. She facilitates that culture of honor in their home as a place where her husband can thrive, flourish and restore after a stressful day of work.

Often, our mother would do this when our dad was arriving home from work. She would excitedly announce to all of us children, "Daddy is almost home from work. Everybody! Let's welcome him home!" We would all be so excited to see our dad and would run from wherever we were to the front door to "surprise" him, trying to be the first one to get to hug or kiss him. No doubt he was tired from a long day at work, but he was always ready and excited to see us after first giving Mama his welcome home kiss. After he had his initial onslaught of happy, little faces and surely, dirty little hands too, Mama would then tell us, "Okay, Daddy's had a long day at work, so let him rest now and change. Maybe he can play with y'all later." Then we'd be summoned to help finish getting dinner on the table or back to our games and antics till called to eat.

The reason for couple time is to rejuvenate and connect on a deeper level. While couple time can take on many forms: dinner out, getting coffee together or just driving around the neighborhood, it's invaluable. It doesn't matter what you're doing but simply that you make intentional time to communicate with each other that you're valuable and care about each other.

Obviously, seasons of life affect this, but no matter what, make time. It's not only good for you as a couple, but it also sets an example to your children and subconsciously communicates to them how to live their lives by priorities. With children, it's ok if they feel second to mamma and daddy. That's a good thing. Don't be afraid to leave them alone or with a sitter for a period of time. It's healthy for the whole family. Couple time is a must for any Proverbs 31 woman to have a happy home. It's almost like going to church once a week as it regroups you and puts you in the right mindset. And don't make an excuse that you can't afford a sitter. Time apart is an investment in your marriage — it's worth paying into that dividend. If nothing else, trade off sitting for friends' children and swap services.

Secret IV - Home

Chapter 20
Health: Invest in the Best, Don't Shortcut Your Home

"She is like the merchants' ships; she bringeth her food from afar." (Prov: 31:14 KJV)

In the time this verse was written, it was common to do trade with foreign nations, and it was also very profitable, but it required a certain amount of understanding of the economy. In the same way, it's interesting to note that a Proverbs 31 woman is compared to a merchant ship. In other words, she is willing to be inconvenienced to gather the choicest foods for her family while also getting a good bargain. A Proverbs 31 woman is able to look beyond her neighborhood to provide for the health of her family — not only to provide culinary delight but also to provide healthy and nutritious foods. Our mother told us that when she was raising us all and my brothers were growing and eating "three times their weight," that she would look at all the grocery store flyers to see the specials of that week and create her menu around them. Extreme times called for extreme measures. She was willing to go to more than one place to find what was nutritious and cost-effective. After all, she had 10 mouths to feed.

In our culture today, we have an increase in disease, illness and sickness. There are a plethora of documentaries supporting this evidence, namely, "In Defense of Food," "What the Health," "Forks Over Knives" and many more. If you look at the health industry, you can see the incline of illness starting when certain drugs were introduced into our eating products, cleaning products and even our healthcare. As a mother, it's important to be aware of these harmful products and know which ones are safe to bring into your home and feed your family. It requires time, knowledge and effort to provide this and a Proverbs 31 woman does just that. Be like a merchant ship. Be willing to travel the distance to provide health and nutrition to your family. If you must, order things online if it's not provided locally. It can be a bit more expensive, but in the long run, you are investing in your health and the health of your family, and there's no price tag you can put on that. Even the richest man would sell all he has for a healthy life. What good is wealth if you're too sick to enjoy it?

Staying up to date on the health scene in today's world is so important, even if you don't have a family and are single. Practice this exercise for yourself so you can use what you learned to bless others and maybe one day your own family. Experiment now in healthy meals to master so you can provide not only healthy but tasty dishes as well.

In addition to getting good deals, this verse also shows that a Proverbs 31 woman pays attention to the broadening expansion of her business endeavors. Just as the merchant's ships would bring fine food and treasures from lands far away, the Proverbs 31 woman would bring her food from afar in her business dealings. No, we don't have to travel to lands far away to buy our food, but she was aware of the cost and willing to pay the price to get the best quality for her household. We should invest in our education, staying updated on the market to get the best products of the highest quality.

As times have changed, so has the definition of what a "keeper at home" means. Before, being a keeper at home meant meal prep, tending to the family, perhaps dabbling in business. It took a lot to run a household back in the day. It was a full-time job because there were no shortcuts like dishwashers, electricity, garbage disposals, laundry rooms, etc. Keeping a house was a lot of work, and it still is. The definition of keeping a home in today's world includes being aware of our health. Society has changed and what we have to be aware of today was not necessarily a concern when this verse was written. Know what products are harmful and not good to bring into your house, which means a lot of reading of labels! There are countless diseases and side effects of chemicals that are affecting us and our children today. As a woman, a mother, a wife, it's imperative that you know and educate yourself about health and the chemicals found in food and cleaning products. Knowledge is power. In this case, ignorance is not bliss. Some great resources are Netflix documentaries, the blog "Eat This Not That," or apps like *Sift* and *ShopWell* that will scan barcodes on food items and tell you the nutritional value and harmful things in the product. It's now easier than ever to educate yourself. Sometimes we need a little help to navigate the food aisle.

Our mother and both of our grandmothers were strong advocates for health. Hardly a day would pass when you wouldn't find our mother reading a book and often times one of them would be health related. She would often relay to us the studies she had recently read and tell us, "Studies show…" and then hit us with some new groundbreaking discovery in the area of health or whatever other book genre she was reading. We often teasingly make fun of her using the quote, "Well, you know, studies do show…". We have been astounded by her wealth of knowledge and how well she stays up to date on the current affairs and advancements, not only in health but in a plethora of other areas. She lived out the old adage: *Readers are leaders and leaders are readers.* Learn and grow and never stop being aware of the constant changes in health concerns in our culture. This is stewarding you and your family's health wisely.

Chapter 21
Hospitality: Serving Messy Oxen

"She riseth also while it is yet night, and giveth meat to her household, and a portion to her maidens." (Prov: 31:15 KJV)

One reason the Proverbs 31 woman was able to do so much was that she had help. She was able to build a support team that helped her create a successful home and, in turn, life. She knew how to leverage the strength and giftings of those in her community. It was not uncommon in middle eastern cultures to leave a lamp burning throughout the night. A woman would rise while it was still dark and replenish the oil and begin her daily tasks to prepare food, grind the corn and prepare the meat to give to her maidens (those helping her) and her family. Getting her rudimentary tasks out of the way early prepared her for the day before the family arose, freed her time up to attend to whatever her occupation was during the day, either as a housewife, vineyard keeper, seamstress, merchant trader, midwife, etc. In modern times, we can easily see this translate to the character of a woman in prepping meals for her family, breakfast, lunch dinner, etc. Thank God for crockpots! The point is that the Proverbs 31 woman was prepared and thought ahead to make time for the other daily tasks she had at hand. We remember well our mother rising early to prepare turkeys for Thanksgiving lunch, staying up late into the night to wrap Christmas presents, and rising early to go out to garage sales to make sure her children had plenty of gifts for Christmas and birthdays.

When hosting a party or gathering, our mother would prepare the table the night before for how she wanted it to be arranged. She thought ahead to make herself available for her guests. She would rise early and put food in the crockpot for different dishes while also labeling each serving dish each item would go into the next morning. There wasn't only the food preparation that was needed but all the equipping, cleaning and getting the house ready (babyproofing certain areas for our guests, if they had little ones). She would always go all out for guests —

cleaning, buying fresh flowers for the table and around the house. She was a woman given to hospitality in every sense of the word and still is. Anything she could do to make it extra nice for her guests, she would do. Phrases such as: "This person loves this chocolate cake so we'll make that" or "This person isn't from the South, so we should serve them some really nice Southern dishes" were quite common days or weeks before guests descended on our home. Even to this day, our mother continues to astound us with her generous heart for hospitality. She has birthed and raised eight babies, and no one could really do that without having the kind of heart she has; and even if she didn't have it before, she'd quickly have to develop it to nurture a family of ten. At the heart of hospitality, there is an attitude of service and a willingness to be prepared so you can serve well. Allow time to prepare for the holidays. Prepare for guests and parties, but realize that the most amazing woman of all had help to make everything happen and oversee it all. Whether you have a housekeeper, mother's helper, family, friend or husband to assist you, it's okay to rest in the fact that you can have help and support.

"Share with the Lord's people who are in need. Practice hospitality." (Romans 12:13 NIV)

This verse on hospitality also backs up Mrs. Proverbs. 31. We'd often have missionaries or Christian brothers and sisters visiting for an extended furlough or acquaintances just driving through town and needed a place to sleep, which, of course, also meant we'd be feeding them as well. There is always room at our table even today. The days of unannounced drop-ins are pretty long gone in our modern culture, but sometimes, we still get them at our house and must quickly accommodate for guests or relatives and set extra plates at the table. That is the heart of a Proverbs 31 women. She's ready and prepared to show hospitality to whoever needs it.

"Where there are no oxen, the manger is empty, but from the strength of an ox come abundant harvests." (Proverbs 14:4 4 NIV)

This proverb paints a perfect picture of the sacrifice needed to make room for abundance. This truth and guiding principle in the woman of valor which we study and desire to emulate also reminds us of a quote by blogger, Sasha Martin of *Global Table Adventure*, "Build bigger tables, not higher fences," or make room for those messy oxen and reap the rewards! We say that laughingly, knowing no one would call their husband, children or house guests messy oxen, but I'm sure they oftentimes may have felt like using it once or twice. Without that sacrifice of service in hospitality, there is no increase or abundance. Hospitality is sacrificial service but reaps great rewards.

Chapter 22
Foresight: Foreseeing the Unseen

"She is not afraid of the snow for her household: for all her household are clothed with scarlet." (Prov:31:21 KJV)

D id you know it typically only snows in Israel (the place this verse was written) two out of every three winters? The snow is typically not long-lasting. However, there have been severe winters in Israel where the snow stayed on the hills of Israel for up to two weeks. It stands out that even though this is still very rare, a verse is dedicated to it. This makes sense because, in ancient times, clothes were one of the only ways one could stay warm, unless you were near hot coals or a burning fire. Understanding that, it makes sense that being clothed in scarlet meant you were well provided for. Scarlet clothing could keep you very warm in cold, inclement weather.

The virtuous woman can think ahead, foresee a need and meet that need before it arrives. This shows her ability to plan ahead and prepare for the future. In today's culture, this can look like saving for a child's tuition for college, a program, braces, etc. Foreseeing that a monetary disaster could arise in the future, she would save up ample amounts of money to be prepared, i.e. in case of famine, having something on hand to meet those needs. She can look at the future and rest knowing she has provided well for her house so when harsh winters of life come, she and her family are provided for.

Christian western culture would have you believe that it is a man's job to provide, but in actuality, the woman is right there alongside her husband, providing as well. The only difference is she understands her unique role in providing as she lives out her life by priorities. Her focus in providing is geared to support the home, so whether you're a single mom or wife and mother, your definition of providing is to nurture the inside of the home, whereas your husband's is geared to providing financial support and focused more outside of the home; but this is a fluid expression that each couple must navigate according to their different seasons of life and within the boundaries of their own specific circumstances.

Our mother was a huge example of this. She would always buy as much food in bulk as she could, yes, to save money, but also to be amply prepared for whatever natural disaster might come our way. She would tell us how her own grandmother would always have her cellar full of canned food for the winter and that you never know when you might be in short supply; those stored foods can save the day.

We have seen that firsthand where we live in Arkansas. As soon as there is a forecast of snow, everybody and their uncle hits the grocery stores. It's amazing how quickly things get sold out as people prepare for the worst: milk, eggs and bread aisles are wiped out in the blink of an eye. Southerners tend to get scared of the snow because we are not as prepared for it as the northern states. We have a bad history of ice storms, specifically in our state and at times have been housebound for days. We were grateful our mother had stocked up beforehand as we lived days bundled up in blankets and eating in candlelight, waiting for the electricity to come back on. But because we were well prepared, those moments were turned into special memories.

In addition to being prepared in the physical, we can also be prepared in the spiritual sense. A part of having foresight and seeing things that are unseen is having spiritual discernment and depth of vision beyond the physical. Moses' wife, Zipporah, had spiritual insight into the situation that her husband put her family in. Because Moses had not obeyed the Lord's command to circumcise his children, the fury of God burned against him and the Lord was ready to kill him (Exodus 4:24-26).

Zipporah had foresight of the perils of her family and resolved the matter, saving her family from the Lord's judgment by circumcising her son and touching Moses' feet with her son's foreskin. This action appeased the Lord's wrath and he turned away his judgment. She took the appropriate action needed and saved her husband and family.

Whether it's preparing for the cold months you don't yet see, or foreseeing a financial strain down the road, or something in which greater spiritual discernment is needed, like in Zipporah's case, the Proverbs 31 woman foresees things before they come upon the scene and takes the necessary action to ensure she and her family are set up for success. She foresees the unseen.

Chapter 23
In tune with Home: Strong Water

"She looketh well to the ways of her household, and eateth not the bread of idleness." (Prov:31:27 KJV)

A virtuous woman is in tune with her husband, her children and the activities of her household. If you're idle and living for yourself, it is hard to be in tune with what is going on around you. Having eight children in our household was no small feat.

> Ellianna: As a little girl, I remember wanting to sit on my father's lap, but he was occupied with my brothers. I remember being sad that he wouldn't hold me and going to my mother to hold me. She had seen what happened and said, "Go again to your daddy and tell him your love language is touch." Being only six or seven years old, I didn't understand what that meant, but I did as she said and my dad responded by picking me up and holding me.

Our mother has a canny way of knowing what others need in a situation and meeting that need. In essence, she is very nurturing. We could tell countless stories of when one of our siblings was going through a difficult season and she would stay up late (losing her sleep) to be there when they came home to just talk. Through this friendship, the Lord used her to speak truth into our siblings' life to get them back on the straight and narrow path. It was a process that took several years, but our sibling eventually came back to the truth. Not everyone's story is like that. Some children take a lifetime to come back to the Lord. Everyone has a different story, but in the case of our mother, her being in tune with the needs of each person in the home made her better able to "look well to the ways of her household." A mother, essentially, is the overseer of the home.

The actions of a woman are like glue between two sheets of paper. It, literally, has the power to hold things together. In the ancient pictograph of the Hebrew word for *mother*, you find two letters making up the word mother: one being "ox" and the second, "water." The Ancient Hebrew Research Center explains it well: "In the original pictographic script, the first letter is a picture of an ox. As the ox is strong, the letter also has the meaning of strong. The second letter represents water. The two letters give us the meaning of 'strong water.'" The Hebrews made glue by boiling animal skins in water. As the skin broke down, a sticky thick liquid formed at the surface of the water. This thick liquid was removed and used as a binding agent, often called "strong water." This is the Hebrew word meaning "mother," the one who "binds the family together."

When a mother is not in tune with her family, it can quickly fall apart. When a woman understands that being in tune with her domain (her household) is one of her main roles as a woman, mother or wife, she looks at her home very differently. Your job is to foster peace and harmony in the home, to provide for the ways of your household in your respective responsibilities. Do this with all diligence. Take time to set decorations out for the holidays; on occasion, turn on music and candles for dinner. Allow time to get organized.

Think of ways you can run your home effortlessly. You can even get your husband and children involved. You are the organizer and facilitator. You are the glue that holds that beautiful mess together. "He that ruleth (let him do it) with diligence." (Romans 12:8 NIV) An Amish Proverb perhaps expounds best on the concept of a mother looking well to the ways of her house:

"A mother is a gardener of God tending to the hearts of her children."

Planting a garden takes work, as does tending to it and watering it. Just like a garden needs order and organization, like a row of plants or flowers in a nice line, so does a well-tended home need order and organization. The fact that this woman "looks well to the ways of her household" communicates intentionality and love toward her home. Even the most beautiful, well-kept of gardens has to go through weeding. She pays attention to its order, wellbeing, function and atmosphere.

She doesn't just work so that her house looks pristine, she also looks at her physical family as little flowers that need nurturing. After all, it is relationships that she is giving time and attention to. Growing up, our mother would always tell us, "A mother can run a happy home by following the *rule of three*: three hugs, three smiles and three praises a day for each person in the home. This is like watering your garden."

Recipe for a Happy Home

The Rule of 3:

Three Hugs

Three Smiles

Three Praises

every day for each person in the home (including your husband) turns a house into a home, a family into friends, and puts love into action.

"The wise woman builds her house, but with her own hands the foolish one tears hers down." (Prov. 14:1 NIV)

One of the most powerful ways to nurture your home or garden is through your words and spirit. Positive words to praise and build up or negative words to destroy and tear down.

Where there is a lack of cleanliness or organization, unkindness or hostility, the atmosphere of a place can feel chaotic and unsettling or restless. The old adage rings true: "A place for everything and everything in its place." Without this sense of order, unease and a feeling of unsettlement takes over. Research indicates that clutter is a hidden culprit that can lead to depression. Who knew how we as woman run our homes can affect the mental and emotional health of our family?

You know those times when your own bedroom is a wreck and it feels like WWII has just broken out? You feel out of control and like you have nothing pulled together. Laundry can be in piles upon piles and mayhem seems to be having its heyday at your house at the cost of your peace of mind and soul. But then, when you finally get things back in order and everything is clean and organized, it's like a calming peace has settled over you and you can enter your room with a sense of joy, accomplishment and sweet contentment. It's like a breath of fresh air.

So it is when a woman tends well to the ways of her household and puts attention and love into her home to create an atmosphere of order, beauty and peace. Even just putting that little vase of fresh flowers on the kitchen table or bedside desk can make everything more beautiful and pleasant.

Why is looking well to the ways of your home coupled with the concept of not being idle? To create this atmosphere of rest and tranquility, we can't eat the bread of idleness. To create this atmosphere of rest, a mother, a woman or grandmother must put forth effort, time, forethought and energy.

Our Mother is an artist who studied interior design in school and has always had an excellent eye to put that time and attention into making our home a place of warmth, peace and beauty. Having eight children didn't afford our house to always be spotless or pristine by a long shot. We got it dirty alright and had fun doing so! Our mother tried to have us children make sure the messes of the day were cleaned before dinner and Dad's arrival.

To make cleaning fun and efficient, our mom would create chore charts and schedules for us to follow and keep on track, so all the work was evenly divided according to the ages of the children. Many fun and joyful memories were made from all the time and attention she invested in our home. The New Testament also shares these same valid truths and a portrait of what Godly womanhood does.

"...teach the young women to be sober, to love their husbands, to love their children, to be discreet, chaste, keepers at home, good, obedient to their own husbands, that the word of God be not blasphemed." (2 Timothy 2:5 KJV)

Looking well to the ways of her household was something Paul taught in his letter to Timothy and the community of faith he led, hundreds of years after the book of Proverbs was written. And that truth still stands today. God's word is judged by the way a woman runs her own home. Her home is to be a reflection of the truth she professes. In fact, her actions and lifestyle themselves are to be what professes the truth she lives by, giving glory and honor to Him who is the ultimate head of her house, Christ Jesus, who is the head of her husband. (Ephesians 5:23)

Chapter 24
Creating Memories

"Her children arise up, and call her blessed; her husband also, and he praiseth her."
(Prov:31:28 NIV)

Sometimes traditions just happen and form, other times they are a result of conscious effort. Our parents made a tradition that after we brought home our Christmas tree, we would all sleep in the living room under the lights of the tree. For Easter, we would watch the same movie (Jesus of Nazareth) every year about the death and resurrection of Jesus. For Thanksgiving, we would read the Thanksgiving story of the pilgrims and put five kernels of corn next to each of our plates, as this was all the pilgrims had during their time of famine. In the year of plenty, to help them remember God's provision and what He had done for them, they set five kernels by their now bountiful plates.

On Valentine's Day, our dad would give us girls a rose and chocolate until the men in our lives came and fulfilled that role. On our birthdays, everyone in the family would go around and share things about the birthday person, describing the things they admired and loved about them. All these things were traditions both our parents upheld. The memories and traditions that our parents gave to us are definitely things for which we all rise up and call her blessed. Truly, memories are the truest and longest lasting gift.

We are so grateful our mother went the extra mile to create memories and traditions for us. Now that many of us are married and have our own families, we have taken many of the same concepts into our own lives. Mother repeatedly would say, "The best gift you can give someone is a memory. That's why we're going to take a vacation this year to____." Our parents invested in memories. Trips and vacations were memories for us. Holiday traditions create stability and are another way of looking well to the ways of your house. Our parents even had special traditions as a couple, such as weekend getaways, anniversary trips, date nights, etc. She made family her priority. It was, and still is, evident in how she lives her life today.

It's amazing how God lines things up perfectly. In the process of writing this portion of the book, our family celebrated Mother's Day. Just like we do for family members on their birthday, we do for our dad on Father's Day and our mother on Mother's Day. We go around and share a word of appreciation and thankfulness about our mother.

This year, all of her children were present, except for the oldest. It changes each year as we have grown as individuals and become more aware of the sacrifices she chose to make (i.e. to raise us and lay down her career in order to homeschool and partner with our dad to raise a family centered on the never changing truths of Jesus Christ and the Word of God and other countless ways she has sacrificed).

Some of us have children now and can praise our mother in a way that is on a different level than before. It's always one of the most precious and beautiful things we love about Mother's Day — to rise up and call her blessed! Our dad will usually go first and speak his praises of our mother, who is his wife of 40 years. We will always take the time to give her the honor and praise she is due. After all, being a mother is a lot of work and deserves a lot of praise!

Secret V - Teacher

"She openeth her mouth with wisdom; and in her tongue is the law of kindness."
(Prov. 31:26 KJV)

"If you can't say something nice, don't say anything at all." Bottom line: let the law of kindness be on your lips at all times. Whenever you share something constructive, it can be from a hardened or annoyed heart or a kind heart. If the motive is for someone's good and is delivered at an appropriate time and manner, then the law of kindness is harnessing your tongue. We grew up with our mother quoting this verse from Proverbs more times than we can count, but she didn't just quote it, she lived it. She isn't perfect, and she'll be the first to admit that, but she is a living example of this principle being walked out daily.

For every one word of correction, she'd try and say at least three or five more words of praise and encouragement, striving to always focus on the positives more than the negatives. We can choose what we will focus on in the people around us, especially family members, as easily as we can choose to use our mouths for building them up or tearing them down. When we were very young, she didn't let her kindness stop her from training or correcting her children, but it was mostly cushioned with affirmation and gentle firmness. Of course, at times, she lost her temper; she's only human. But she was always quick to ask for forgiveness. And that action taught us the heart of kindness.

We have often wondered how she can choose to focus on the good in someone when all we want to do is focus on their problems and shortcomings, but just as love is a choice, so is the way we view someone's strengths and weaknesses. They do not control our opinion of them. We do. Jesus could have had the right to spew hatred and condemnation on his murderers, but even on the cross, beaten beyond recognition, he prayed, "Father, forgive them for they know not what they do." That kind of love, that heart of kindness that trumped the law of sin and death, is the same law that binds the Proverbs 31 woman's lips.

She has been kissed by love itself, Jesus, and her mouth is forever sealed by its sweet and eternal taste, better than life itself. She has been so touched by the Father's law of kindness that her own words and lips are changed by it before she even opens her mouth to speak.

"Death and life are in the power of the tongue: and they that love it shall eat the fruit thereof." (Proverbs 18:21 KJV)

She can speak life or death with the choice and attitude of her words. This verse comes to her often when she opens her mouth, for she knows it can build up or tear down. A woman can build up her home with her own words and attitudes.

"A woman's family is held together by her wisdom, but it can be destroyed by her foolishness." (Proverbs 14:1 CEV)

Part of being a "Woman Arising" is that she arises into the identity and authority she has over her home and uses her power to build up instead of destroy. She teaches not only with her words but also in how she lives her life. If ties between you and your family are strained, realize you have the power and ability to build them up again simply by the wisdom you impart in both action, deed and manner of your words. Kindness is the cheapest and sometimes most costly gift to give. Let your whole life be a lesson plan in wisdom and kindness.

Chapter 25
Exuding Wisdom: Become a Learner, a Reader, a Leader

"Wisdom is the principal thing; therefore get wisdom: and with all thy getting get understanding." (Prov 4:7 KJV)

"Study to show thyself approved..." (2 Timothy 2:15 KJV)

Have you ever heard the saying, "Leaders are readers and readers are leaders"? If you want to lead, then read. As a mother, a wife, a friend, a woman, we are all in positions to lead and advise others. Did you know a woman is to assume the role of a teacher? It is very clear in 1 Timothy 2:12 that a woman is not to teach men or assume a leadership role of teaching over them. And yet, we see that Priscilla, with her husband Aquila, expounds on the gospel to a new believer named Apollos (Acts 18:24-26). We also see the role of teacher that women were to faithfully teach other women, specifically about how to do good, (Titus 2:3-5), with an emphasis on the older women teaching the younger women.

This is why it's imperative that we make sure that what we study and learn is something of wise counsel. It was rare to find our mother without something in her hand helping her learn: a book, magazine, article, cassette tapes, etc. In order to teach about something, you have to be knowledgeable in that area. A virtuous woman is a reader. She takes time to study and learn before she teaches. You can't have wisdom without reading. How can a mother be the glue and binding force of the family if she does not take the time to learn and grow? Do you have something in the Bible you want to learn more about? Then read! Study and learn. In so doing, you will show yourself approved and exude wisdom.

"By wisdom a house is built, and through understanding it is established; through knowledge its rooms are filled with rare and beautiful treasures." (Proverbs 24:3-4 NIV)

Growing up, the word of God was woven into the fabric of our everyday lives and grounded every topic of learning. When our parents decided to homeschool their children, they planned to have about 6 or 8 children, as the Lord blessed them. They were involved with a homeschool curriculum that approached academics through a Biblical lens. Through this homeschooling group, they got the idea to have a daily family devotion called "wisdom search." In these "wisdom searches," we would all go around and take turns reading through the Bible together every morning, searching to glean of its wisdom. Many times, our dad would already be off to work when all the children were fed and clothed for the day so the "wisdom searches" would mostly be led by our mom. She would make it engaging and interactive for us children by storybooks, acting out what she was reading, singing songs to help us remember Scripture, etc. Even today, the teaching she taught us still guides us in our decision making.

In essence, the searching of wisdom was a part of our daily life and we were taught at a young age to go to the Bible to fill the rooms of our minds with the word of God. We now know these rooms and chambers of our hearts and minds manifest positively in our homes. The ancient proverb rings true:

"For as he thinks in his heart, so is he." (Proverbs 23:7 NKJV)

The word of God trains you how to think about God, yourself, and life itself. In our "wisdom searches," we were learning about God — He who is Wisdom Himself. It was with the source of all wisdom (as revealed in Scripture) that the rooms of our house were filled!

Wisdom can arrive in a variety of ways: through experience, conversations with others, observing other's successes and failures. But, perhaps, the best way to absorb wisdom is through reading. As you read and learn more, you store up vats of wisdom and understanding. But where is wisdom found? If it's so coveted, where can we find it? Remember, one of the descriptions of virtuous is wise. Wisdom is definitely something a Proverbs 31 woman has in abundance.

Therefore, when she opens her mouth to answer a question or instruct, it will be filled with what was digested through learning and studying. While learning from what others have to say is important, perhaps one thing that's more important is to go to the ultimate source of wisdom, which is the word of God.

"For the LORD gives wisdom, and from his mouth come knowledge and understanding." (Proverbs 2:6 NIV)

We can let authors be our mentors and friends and teach us things they have learned alongside truths taught in the Bible. Like we mentioned, our mother is never without a book. Whenever she takes road trips, she always has a "book bag." Late at night, she would be reading about health, how to be a good wife and mother, parenting books, etc. Because she reads, she always has something to share on just about any topic. Whenever we were stopped at a light or waiting in a doctor's office, she'd always have a book in her satchel, ready to read. The books she'd read would typically be books on spirituality, health, business or relationships.

How often we turn to our phone is how often our mother turned to books. She was constantly reading; therefore, she was constantly learning. Wisdom gives you understanding in just about every topic of life. To be a woman who exudes wisdom — read and study.

Always have a book you are reading to improve yourself. Unlike articles, books give you a sense of accomplishment. Completing a book gains a certain level of respect from others about your opinion on a certain topic. For example, if you try to tell someone about Jesus and they ask if you have read the Bible and you can answer yes, then you are considered more of an authority on the topic of Jesus as opposed to if you haven't read it.

The same is true in all seven areas of our womanhood. Make it a goal to read at least seven books each year, one that fits in each category. Some can read seven books at a time while others need to concentrate on *one* book at a time. Find what works for you and get started. Ask God to whet your appetite as a learner, and if you're not already a big reader, watch Him take you to new heights in all seven areas.

What the Lord will reveal to one person may not be the same thing He reveals to another. With that humility and wisdom, our mother was unashamed to glean from the wisdom of others. In fact, it is wisdom itself to go to others and seek out wisdom from those who are wise. (Prov. 11:14)

Our mother followed this pattern of seeking wisdom as it is laid out in Scripture but also through books. She would implement tips or research she had learned, incorporated with the timeless truth of the Word of God, into filling the rooms of our house with her findings. She was always gathering and amassing more wisdom, "gleaning from the field" as it were, and weighing it with Scripture. Because she was always reading and growing, she had wisdom at the tip of her tongue ready to answer the many eager questions from her eight children at various stages of life, and this wisdom continues today. We attribute her diligence in this as a huge contributing factor to the success of the house our parents built together.

Unless the learner becomes the teacher, the teacher can never lead. As Scripture instructs, out of the abundance of the heart, the mouth speaks. As Proverbs 31 women, let us take the time to fill our hearts with the wisdom and the knowledge of God so then we can instruct those under our care with influence and excellence. Learn so you can teach, teach so you can lead, lead so you can influence the world for Christ.

Chapter 26
Law of Kindness: It's in God's DNA

"She openeth her mouth with wisdom; and in her tongue is the law of kindness." (Prov. 31:26 KJV)

"Or do you show contempt for the riches of his kindness, forbearance and patience, not realizing that God's kindness is intended to lead you to repentance?" (Romans 2:4 NIV)

Not only is kindness one of the fruits of the Spirit, it is also one of the main fruits evidenced that someone is a Proverbs 31 woman. But what is the Law of kindness? What does this fruit look like? The word "law" mentioned here is the Hebrew word for "torah," which commonly refers to the first five books of the Bible, the Law of Moses. But most of us don't think of the Torah as the book of kindness. We typically think about laws and God's judgment, not kindness. But this is where a woman's perspective comes in, to teach and expound on the kindness factor of the law.

For example, starting all the way back in Genesis, God created a perfect world for man and woman where they could live eternally with Him in perfect peace and harmony — a world without sin, pain and famine. But God, in his love and kindness, gave humankind free will to choose whether to live or not. Love is the ability to choose.

As the Scriptures say, Adam and Eve chose to sin by eating of the forbidden tree. God, in His mercy, took away the tree of eternal life so that humans would not have to live in sin forever. That was kind. True to God's character, He redeemed the situation so that they could once again be in perfect peace with Him through death, the death of His Own Son. That's why it is so powerful that Christ conquered death because it was the enemy's attempt to usurp the perfect world God created for mankind. God, in his love and kindness, redeemed and showed grace.

The Lord commands us to be courteous to one another. As being courteous and having manners are just acts of kindness lived out every day; it's been said that "Relationships are built on little acts of kindnesses."

"Finally, be ye all of one mind, having compassion one of another, love as brethren, be pitiful, be courteous." (1 Peter 3:8)

A Proverbs 31 woman can be courteous and kind by esteeming others higher than themselves and by showing deference and by being compassionate. All these are contributing factors of kindness. To practically live out kindness is to have manners and be courteous. So, it could be more accurate to say a Proverbs 31 woman has manners, kindness and graciousness on her tongue at all times.

"Manners are just learned kindnesses," our great grandmother would always tell our mother. Mother took that nugget of wisdom to heart and taught it to us while we were growing up, leading by example. To this day, because of the good manners she taught us, and practicing the law of courtesy, honor and respect, people often ask: "How do you know how to do that?" as if our behavior is out of the norm. To us, it's not abnormal thankfulness or gratitude but excellent training and teaching from our mother.

A practical way our Mother taught us to be kind was by asking us to take a few thank you notes in our suitcase whenever we travel, because there are always those situations that arise where you want to take the time to express a special thank you to a host of an event, schedule coordinator or someone hosting you in their home. And, of course, you don't go to a dinner engagement without offering to bring something to contribute to the meal or visit someone's home for dinner the first time without bringing some kind of a hostess gift: (wine, plant, or a candle) or even visit a new neighbor without bringing a housewarming gift. There are a million ways to show honor and respect according to your own nation's norms and cultures' protocol that exudes kindness. You learn how to love and honor them in the way they understand. Even Paul Himself knew this:

"For though I am free from all men, I have made myself a servant to all, that I might win the more... I have become all things to all men, that I might by all means save some. Now this I do for the gospel's sake..." (1 Cor. 9:19, 22-23 NKJV)

Paul understood the importance of submitting himself to a culture's understanding of honor and respect to bring them to a higher understanding of the Kingdom culture that supersedes all earthly norms. The Kingdom of Heaven is founded on honor and respect, so the way one person understands honor, or a culture understands it, should be learned so that we might show the love and kindness of God in a way they can understand.

When our family did missionary work in Romania for three years, we learned the importance of accommodating to a culture in order to transform it. We did not let their culture ever dictate the culture of the Kingdom in us, but we became acquainted with their culture in order to facilitate open doors and the sharing of the Gospel.

God is good and kind and, therefore, good manners are Godly because they teach you how to show kindness to a specific person or people group. So, this whole thing about Mrs. Proverbs 31 having the law of kindness is basically saying that she shows the kindness, honor and character of Christ in all her ways.

She not only shows it, but she teaches it to those in her sphere of influence by her example and teaching. She lets God's Kingdom values trump her own cultural norms.

Think of the "Good Samaritan." He wasn't just kind to a stranger, he went above and beyond the cultural norms of his society. In fact, he even overstepped them by reaching out to a poor Jewish man. As a Samaritan, he was looked down on and was a despised enemy of the Jews. He far exceeded any social obligation or cultural norm, and at great personal sacrifice, tended to this man who should have been cared for by his own people, the ones who saw him in need but did nothing. (Luke 10:25-37) That story is kindness itself: going out of one's way to attend to and make others feel honored and valued. The good Samaritan did that in abundance.

Jesus also taught this when he said, *"Go the extra mile"* (Matt 5:41) and *"Bless your enemies and those that curse you."* (Luke 6:28) There is a cultural norm of kindness and goodness, but as a child of the Kingdom, not of this Earth, a Proverbs 31 woman, far surpasses what is expected. She is bound to a higher law, the law of love and kindness. Outrageous kindness and unheard-of-goodness are her norms because she is not normal. She is of another Kingdom and lives out that unique brand of kindness.

We've met certain believers who walk in this kind of godly goodness that defies the normal standard for good; the kind of goodness no one else would trouble themselves with because the cost is too great. This kind of selfless love and undeserved kindness is the definition of an excellent woman, the one of whom it is said, "Who can find her?"

The book of Exodus goes on to discuss God's law of kindness, especially when we look at the 10 commandments and how God tells us how to treat others, explicitly in His moral laws laid out on murder, theft, adultery, integrity toward others and honesty. Upon reading those laws, you find the heart of kindness in them. (Exodus 20 and 21) And this is where a Proverbs 31 woman's perception is to come into play: to teach others about the kindness of the Savior. In fact, The Psalms explains the makeup of God as being full of lovingkindness:

"How precious is Your lovingkindness, O God! And the children of men take refuge in the shadow of Your wings." (Psalm 36:7 KJV)

Kindness is at the heart of who God is. To be a virtuous Proverbs 31 woman who has the law of kindness on her tongue, we have to understand that all of God's laws are wrapped up in this: "Love your neighbor as yourself." And in so doing, we fulfill the law of Christ! This is truly the law of kindness: "Carry each other's burdens, and in this way, you will fulfill the law of Christ (Galatians 6:2)." To be a teacher of the law of kindness, the Proverbs 31 woman saturates herself with the word of God (and especially the Torah) so that God's kind laws overflow into all her conversations without a second thought.

Just like the verse for this chapter states, it's God's *kindness* that leads us to repentance. Repentance means walking in a new direction, the opposite from the direction you walked before. When we were sinners, we walked in a way not given to kindness. Our sinful nature just wants to be selfish. The Proverbs 31 woman teaches that because of the kindness shown to us by God, we must show kindness to others.

In the book "Tortured for Christ," Richard Wurmbrand tells of a remarkable story of the kindness of God wooing the heart of a sinner to salvation. Richard had been meeting with Romanian communists, and one of the young communist soldiers got saved when he read a story about the kindness of Jesus toward his disciples. The young man said he had never witnessed kindness like that and could hardly imagine the reality of a superior showing kindness to a subservient. That concept was not in the communist culture he had been raised in. He said it was the kindness of Jesus that led him to give his life to Christ!

Such extraordinary and radical kindness is not the culture we have been raised in either. We were all born sinners and it is still the sinful flesh that doesn't want to be kind and considerate to others. This is all the more reason that kindness and manners need to be taught by mothers and fathers, and those under our care, but especially the Proverbs 31 woman because a mother influences the way the next generation thinks and behaves. The kindness we show, live out and teach, is to point others to the kindness of God and much like the Romanian soldier, woo us to His bosom.

Chapter 27
Teaching the Younger: Love is the Best Teacher

"These commandments that I give you today are to be on your hearts. Impress them on your children. Talk about them when you sit at home and when you walk along the road, when you lie down and when you get up." (Deut 6:6-7 NIV)

Secret V says a Proverbs 31 woman is a teacher. While there are many spheres to what and how to teach, perhaps there is no teaching position more powerful and influential than the role of a mother. A mother is a teacher, especially when a child is very young and a dependent infant. She constantly gives herself to maintaining and upholding the life of her child. A mother teaches not only by doing but by being present. Never underestimate the power of presence.

> Melissa: I was a nanny for 3 ½ years and probably have spent that same amount of time, or more, in just babysitting here and there throughout the years for friends and family. Especially with infants, you can see their total dependency on their mother. If they don't see her in the room the little baby will often scan the room, searching for her 'til they see her face. When she leaves the room, there's often that displeasure and lack of peace, sometimes expressed in tears or crying. I'm sure most of us have witnessed this. A mother does have to teach her child to be okay without her at times, especially as they grow older, but studies show the most formative years of a person are formed in the first seven years of life.

How does a mother, or any woman teach? It is by how she "shows" what she teaches and by her very presence. She doesn't only tell her child to be loving, she herself is loving. A child will do what you do more than what you say. The old saying rings true: "Do what I say, not what I do." Many tell their child to do something and then go and do the exact opposite. No doubt this is why we have this familiar phrase.

The most powerful way of teaching the truth is by demonstrating it; more is caught than taught.

"This is how we know what love is: Christ gave his life for us. We too, then, ought to give our lives for others!" (1 John 3:16 GNT)

We know what love is because it was demonstrated to us by Jesus. He had to show us what love looked like for us to know it. The same is true for anyone teaching anything. Man or woman, young or old, we all teach by showing. God Himself taught us what love is by showing it through His Son, Jesus, and giving Him up for us. Jesus' incarnation in the flesh had to happen in order for this to be demonstrated to us.

A mother's presence with her children allows her to show what love is and what it does. Teaching by showing and the giving of your own presence is not just for a mother-child relationship but can be with any woman working with younger children, or even those who do not have children. This example of teaching by demonstrating that we see in the Proverbs 31 woman transcends women in all walks of life and in all season of life. All who are around her are taught as she manifests the character of Christ. This could be in a business or professional setting or at home. Whatever setting it is in, the tone and expression of love are set, although it may take on different outward forms and expressions. Another key verse in bringing this "teaching" role of an excellent woman into focus is:

"Dear children, let's not merely say that we love each other; let us show the truth by our actions."

(1 John 318 NLT)

People often say something is "easier said than done." Love cannot be silent or sit on the sidelines because love will pay whatever cost necessary. The word says God is love. He saw what was needed for humankind and paid the highest cost of giving up His own Son for us. Sometimes, love does something by choosing inaction or silence, as in the situation of Jesus before His accusers, but that very choice to not do something is just as much an action as anything else — perhaps even more so. Sometimes, inaction is the action most needed.

One of the highest expressions of sacrificial love is a woman giving up her body and laying it down to bear a child. She has to sacrifice her own life, her body and freedoms to give life to another. There is pain in childbirth, and it is a bloody mess, literally, but that is what love does. It sacrifices for another and on occasion, blood is shed. Just as Christ shed his blood to bring new life for humankind, so does a woman sheds her blood to bring new life into the world. It's a beautiful picture, no matter whether you have ten children, one child, or none at all. Yet, again, we see the role of a mother teaching what love is because she can give of herself like no other; laying down her life for nine months and ending in the climax of labor.

Our maternal great grandmother said, "You shouldn't have children if you're not going to raise them. Some people just don't raise their children." If you bear a child, you are responsible for the rearing and training of that child and teaching them in the ways of the Lord.

"Train up a child in the way he should go, and when he is old he will not depart from it." (Proverbs 22:6 KJV)

Our own parents took that verse seriously and made it a primary focus to train us in the ways of the Lord, always encouraging each child according to their own unique gifts and talents.

"These commandments that I give you today are to be on your hearts. Impress them on your children. Talk about them when you sit at home and when you walk along the road, when you lie down and when you get up." (Deut 6:6-7 NIV)

Never did a day pass when God or His word was not a topic in our home, conversation or practice.

Since the book of Proverbs specifically commands children to not forsake the teaching of their mothers (Proverbs 1:8), the most obvious way a woman can be a teacher and teach the law of kindness is to the audience of her own children. If you do not have your own physical children, then what spiritual children do you have who you could counsel and advise? You might have younger friends or family members that could take the place of child in that they are someone who you can influence. Since Proverbs commands children to not forsake the teaching of their mothers, it seems to be implying that mothers (or women filling that role in their lives) are their primary appointed teachers. So, is a woman supposed to be a teacher? You better believe it! The word also says in Titus:

"the older women likewise" are to, *"admonish the young women to love their husbands, to love their children, to be discreet, chaste, homemakers, good, obedient to their own husbands, that the word of God may not be blasphemed."* (Titus 2:3-5 NKJV)

In essence, no matter your exact role or title, or the age of those in your sphere of influence, a woman carries the call of being a "mother," caretaker and nurturer for those in her midst and teaches all by her example and presence.

Secret VI – Business

"But thou shalt remember the LORD thy God: for it is he that giveth thee power to get wealth, that he may establish his covenant which he sware unto thy fathers, as it is this day." (Duet 8:18 KJV)

In addition to being a teacher, the Proverbs 31 woman was an astute businesswoman. Business is the most talked about subject in all of Proverbs 31. Perhaps because modern day Christian women need a mind shift of what a biblical businesswoman looks like. We often tend to think we have to choose between business or family, business or ministry. But Proverbs 31 gives us a different perspective on business.

Business is a vehicle to point others to God, serve our family and do the kingdom work God has set before us. It's not choosing one over the other, it's living a balanced life with our priorities in place knowing when to choose family over business. But that business can also be a support and blessing to family and ministry. We strive to be successful in business to point others to Christ not only in how we run our business and how we invest but also in who we can bless from our businesses.

Business is also a way to teach your children about finances, taxes, budgeting and just financial principles in general. Business does not have to be separate from family, it can be integrated. One business that took on this mindset is Sam Walton, founder of Walmart. Our grandfather and grandmomma Bailey took several vacations with the Waltons.

Sam, a fellow Arkansan, was good friends with our grandparents and would share his philosophies about life and business with them. Mr. Walton was a down to earth man, no pretenses. He would always drive a well-loved or used truck and wear overalls. Yet, he had one of the most successful business ever. His secret? Do what's right. He said people needed discounted items and he wanted to provide that. Along with his family, he started what is now the famous Walmart store.

His mindset about business isn't far off from how the Jewish community runs their family businesses. And since Proverbs 31 was written about a Jewish woman, it would stand to reason to understand their mindset on business: family and business go hand in hand. In the

Jewish mindset, wealth is something every family should strive for. Because the more wealth you have, the more you can bless others.

To understand this verse for secret six, we have to go back to the Hebrew text which translates the word *"wealth"* differently. It has more of the connotation of abundance in all things.

The Hebrew word here used for wealth is "Chayil," pronounced Hi Eel, which means virtue, valor, might, strength. Interesting to note is that the same word is used in Proverbs 31:10: *"Who can find a virtuous woman?"* Or paraphrased: *"Who can find a woman who brings abundance, wealth, health - Abundance in all things including wealth."* That's a tall order!

The heart of any business or career should point others to the knowledge of God and to bless others. To understand God's heart about business is to also understand what His covenant was with Israel, since He obviously said their prosperity in wealth was for the purpose of establishing that covenant with them.

Part of God's covenant with Israel was the promise of property, physical land (i.e. the land of Canaan that became the nation of Israel). Another part of God's covenant with Abraham was the promise to make a great nation out of him and his offspring through whom all the families of the Earth would be blessed. God also wanted to make the Israelites a strong and flourishing people to show forth His goodness and glory to all people that would abound in His lavish blessings and goodness toward them to showcase the blessings of the Lord, "which make rich." (Prov 10:22)

In essence, God wanted to put a family, a people, on display as those who are more outrageously blessed than any others. This was not because of their own goodness or greatness; in fact, it was in spite of it. He made this covenant so all the earth would know and see what kind of a God He is. God identified Himself as the God of Israel. So, their walking in blessings or curses, in a way, was a direct correlation of His relationship with them. How His children prosper show what kind of Father and God He is. God cares a lot about His reputation on the Earth. (Deut 7:6-9)

Though it may sound strange, God is the perfect business "man," perfect manager and Master. He governs over an entire universe and galaxy after galaxy, maybe even multiple universes, some have speculated! *"The increase of His government has…no end…"* (Isa. 9:7 KJV)

God is zealous over all things in His government. The word for zeal in the NLT puts it as "passionate commitment!" That means He is passionate and committed to all the things under His domain. He longs and works to establish justice and righteousness not just now but for eternity. Business is a formalized venue where humans can see that being practiced and manifested. What if it was totally normal to see the Kingdom of God invading Earth in the marketplace or in your own business? What if God's business principles were the norm? What a different business environment we'd live in today.

Business is a venue to execute the Father's business of pursuing justice and seeking freedom for the oppressed and poor, both physically and spiritually. Poverty is often the work of Satan, for God died for us to have abundance in all areas of our lives. As sons and daughters of God, we are called to carry that abundant life into every area and sphere of influence we have. What an exciting, epic adventure God invites us into!

"For the creation waits in eager expectation for the children of God to be revealed. For the creation was subjected to frustration, not by its own choice, but by the will of the one who subjected it, in hope that the creation itself will be liberated from its bondage to decay and brought into the freedom and glory of the children of God." (Romans 8:19-21 NIV)

And what is the business of our Father, the Creator of all things? He tells us plainly in His word:

"The Spirit of the Sovereign LORD is on me, because the LORD has anointed me to proclaim good news to the poor. He has sent me to bind up the brokenhearted, to proclaim freedom for the captives and release from darkness for the prisoners." (Isaiah 61:1 NIV)

To co-create with the Creator is a sheer honor. God desires His children to partner with Him in bringing abundant life, and to take His glory and excellence into every assignment He sends us to. We all have strengths and weaknesses that often become more pronounced in the business arena. We encourage you, whether you own your business, work for a business, or have dominion in other platforms outside of business, to remember that God will work through you because of the unique way He created you in spite of your weaknesses.

Satan has tried to tempt us to compare ourselves with one another in various ways, and we have to be quick to put his lies and thoughts to death and bring each thought under the authority of Jesus, as the word tells us to do. This verse especially has encouraged us in the area of business but also in working with God:

"For those who are led by the Spirit of God are the children of God. The Spirit you received does not make you slaves, so that you live in fear again; rather, the Spirit you received brought about your adoption to sonship. And by him we cry, 'Abba, Father.'... Now if we are children, then we are heirs—heirs of God and co-heirs with Christ, if indeed we share in his sufferings in order that we may also share in his glory." (Romans 8:14-17 NIV)

Doing business *with* God is something we do out of daughterhood, as His children. Knowing this can help us to rest in the Lord, knowing that our good Father will be running the business, and all we have to do is listen to Him and we'll grow it together. Working with a loving and perfect dad is *fun*, not scary! Yes, you do have to work, but it's something that gives you joy and is not just monotonous repetition because you're getting to do it with your dad and He's helping you. Business is a partnership with God, just like Jesus told His disciples:

"I no longer call you servants, because a servant does not know his master's business. Instead, I have called you friends, for everything that I learned from my Father I have made known to you." (John 15:15 NIV)

As you step out in faith to grow your business, you'll be stepping more deeply into your identity of daughterhood with Him, and He'll help you grow in excellence and will perfect the character of Christ in you as a testimony for all to see the blessing of the Lord lived out through you.

Whatever business God has called you to is also your mission field, for no business can grow outside of a relationship with human people. Every relationship is an open door for us to show and manifest the glory and beauty of God. And even if you aren't dealing with people directly, day-to-day, in your business, your business, in some form or fashion, directly or indirectly, affects people.

Chapter 28
The Value of Toil and Reward

"She seeketh wool, and flax, and worketh willingly with her hands." (Prov 31:13 KJV)

The Proverbs 31 woman most likely produced her own wool and flax from her investments. Therefore, it would make sense that she would use her earnings from those investments to make garments for the household, taking care of both her family's inner and outer needs. To fully understand this verse, we'll need to understand what it is talking about. When it was written, flax and wool were the tools necessary to make garments. It was not uncommon for women to make their own clothes. Wool was typically used as outer clothing and flax (used to make linen) typically used for undergarments.

The fact that she "worketh willingly with her hands" denotes she was willing, yes, but that it pleased her to work with her hands. This woman was not afraid of working hard because she understood the value of "toil and reward." She enjoyed seeing the fruit of her hand bring a profit and found joy in providing for her family in that way.

She was enthusiastic and intentional in her work. Other translations translate this verse saying she works with "eager hands" or with "delight." In essence, she is talented with the tools at her disposal. Know the tools God has given you. Ask Him even now what tools He's given you. If you need to grow in learning how to use a new tool, learn it. Your tool today may not be wool and flax, but you can still work willingly with your hands and your mind, after all, the Lord said to love Him with "all your heart, all your soul and all your mind." (Luke 10:27) Use everything and anything to diligently work for the Lord and contribute to the life of your family and those in need. Keep growing and expanding your ability to serve the Lord in new ways. Grow the Lord's business with Him and be intentional in giving Him the best.

Invest in yourself so you can invest well into your business and others. Work hard, be creative to provide an increase for your family that will provide both for the physical needs and private needs of your household. Good business meets a need. The Proverbs 31 woman found a need and met it both by providing for the needs of the merchants in the streets and clothing for her household.

Chapter 29
Income Contributor: Growing Wealth from Your Earnings

"She considereth a field, and buyeth it: with the fruit of her hands she planteth a vineyard." (Prov 31:16 KJV)

Before we delve into all that the Proverbs 31 woman does to be an income contributor to the home, we have to dispel the nonsense that women shouldn't work. We grew up among many peers who had the notion and idea that a woman should not work outside the home but should solely be a "keeper at home." However, when you really study the Bible and delve into the truths laid out before us, you see this position is unsupportable.

With that said, confusion over a woman's role comes when she doesn't know how to live her life by priorities. A powerful woman is one who knows her unique design and role in life and can live her life according to those priorities. We desire for women to move away from judging one another about the choices we make, whether to only work at home or outside the home. Both choices are biblical as long as we do it through our priorities.

Ellianna: I recently was at a women's conference where the speaker had a room of about 200 ladies write down what fears they faced. The common theme was fear of judgment, of what others think of us because we're not perfect, we may fail, we may be rejected, or we may not be good enough. My heart broke as I saw the common thread of judgmental attitudes holding women back. Many felt they couldn't do certain things because they felt they would be judged by other Christian women. How sad.

As we'll look in a moment, you'll see that a Proverbs 31 woman is a woman who is very business minded; she's out and about working and making deals happen. This can look a myriad of ways, but the point is that the Proverbs 31 woman is free to do business without judgment because she also manages her home well. If you are a woman struggling to manage your home and do business, that's okay; take a step back and regroup. Many women struggle with keeping the right balance. None of us knows someone else's circumstances, therefore, we should not judge each other.

Our hope and desire from this section is this: if you are a homemaker and not involved in business in some way, we hope this encourages you to be an income contributor; if you are a career woman, however, and not home very often with your family, may this encourage you to consider possibly making some changes to allow you to be a woman who aligns her life with the principles outlined in Proverbs 31.

We all have times and seasons where we become imbalanced due to life circumstances and that's okay. Everyone has an "ox in the ditch" scenario/season now and then. The key is finding your way back to the equilibrium point — the way of the Proverbs 31 woman. Both the income contributor and homemaker are Proverbs 31 women. Our challenge to you is to find an equilibrium that allows room for both. One of our favorite sayings is, "The key to the Christian life is balance." The rest of this chapter will look at the practical ways and principles a Proverbs 31 woman uses to incorporate business into her everyday life.

Now that we've established a woman's appointed role in business, let's look at how she deals in business. The verse for this section, Proverbs 31:16, shows a woman who is methodical and not rash in her business dealings. She considers the value of something and makes a wise and smart purchase. She does so from her previous hard labor. With the fruit of her hands, she plants a vineyard: another business venture that not only grows her income but provides for her family's needs and gives her the ability to bless others. This takes forethought and knowledge; she has a good scope of the land and the running value of a piece of property before investing in it. She is knowledgeable and educated about her business ventures.

This verse denotes several business principles that are still relevant today, principles that transcend culture, time and race. The principles are:

1) The Proverbs 31 woman "considers" her investments. She is not an impulsive buyer and takes time to research and weigh the pros and cons. Nothing considered over time carries remorse, only that done in haste brings great sorrow. In other words, haste makes waste! A godly businesswoman takes her time before she wheels and deals in business. After careful consideration, she advances and moves to the next phase in business. This is contrary to the business culture of today which pushes the mindset of now or never.

2) From the fruit of her hands, or from her "earnings," she plants a vineyard. This principle implies that the Proverbs 31 woman does not go into debt to try and build wealth quickly. Instead, she takes time and when she sees her investment is good, she takes her earnings to buy another profitable field, or in today's terms, a profitable business investment. She is a wise and shrewd businesswoman. She carefully invests her earnings in order to yield a great return. Having a vineyard in ancient times required a lot of work and dedication. Her undertaking was no small feat.

To apply this to today's world, consider your business/career decisions prayerfully and deliberately. Weigh the pros and cons, and don't rush into anything. Consider what business/career is before you and before moving ahead ask yourself, "Will any of the other priorities outlined in this book be sacrificed?" Once you see that your decision is profitable, invest your earnings so you can provide for the needs of your house and those in the business world and move toward being financially independent.

When faced with a crossroads decision, consider this: "If I choose this, will I still be living according to the Proverbs 31 woman's ancient secrets?" If the answer is yes, then you can have peace of mind to move forward. If, however, your husband, children and house suffer at the expense of you moving ahead in a career choice or business investment, and your answer is no, then stop and reconsider. (Jeremiah 6:16)

Chapter 30
Quality Investments

"She perceived that her merchandise is good: her candle goeth not out by night."
(Prov 31:18 KJV)

T o understand the Biblical principles of finance, we have to understand one principle: your personal finances are not yours to begin with, they are God's. Everything we have is from Him (1 Chronicles 29:14). Guess what topic Jesus spoke on the most outside of the Kingdom of God? That's right, money! Almost half of His parables have to do with finances. Perhaps this is because humans struggle the most with how to manage, use and spend money. Business, finance and money are definitely important topics to God. Whether you own your own business or just manage your own personal finances, it's hard to be successful and have financial peace and gain financial independence unless you understand how God sees finances.

Some people find this discouraging because they feel like God is more concerned with their finances than He is with their hearts. Let's be clear, the Bible says, "Man looks at the outward, but God looks at the heart." (I Sam 16:7JKV) So your heart is much more important to God than your wallet. However, with that said, there isn't much separation between a person's heart and their wallet.

Dave Ramsey, founder of Financial Peace University and an expert in financial habits, put it this way when referring to people and their first credit cards, "People are emotionally attached to money." It's no doubt there is a need for financial counseling in America. People find it challenging to know how to view money and wealth.

To one, God may say, "Go and build a multi-million-dollar business" and to another, He may say, "Go, sell all you have and follow me," much like He told the disciples. Since business flows out of the partnership with God, He has the prerogative to tell one of His children to "Go here," and another to "Go there." As our dad says, "A servant serves and does whatever His master tells Him to. He doesn't get caught up in what he is doing, but rather in obeying and serving His master." We know people who have been extremely successful in business and God told them to give it all away and follow Him in a new and different path. Our father lived this out when he was about to be promoted after ten years of work at his job but had heard the call to missionary work. As a family, we left for Romania before he received his promotion. This decision to accept God's call instead of personal gain made a big impact on us as teenagers. It will be different for each of us, but what God desires most is obedience. Obedience is the best way. Whatever the Lord is leading you to do with your finances, whether it be following the word of God or the Spirit's guidance, obeying His leadership is the best way.

We cannot tell you what He wants you to do with your finances, but the Bible can and does. Even if you don't have direct guidance on certain finances under your control, you always have the word of God. And that is our main source of knowing what the Father's will is. To make money and to give money are both Biblical. Perhaps John Wesley, the famous minister from the eighteenth century puts it best: "Earn all you can, give all you can, save all you can." How much, how little you ask? Let that be determined by your personal relationship with God and the study of His word.

Renowned author Peter Grandich said his years as a highly successful Wall Street stockbroker left him spiritually depleted and clinically depressed. He also said the Bible is an excellent financial advisor, whether or not you're religious. "I get my financial guidance from the Bible," Grandich said, author of *Confessions of a Wall Street Whiz Kid*. He goes on to say, "Money and possessions are the second most referenced topic in the Bible – money is mentioned more than 800 times – and the message is clear: nowhere in Scripture is debt viewed in a positive way."

Former New York Giants player Lee Rouson and author Peter Grandich co-founded Trinity Financial Sports & Entertainment Management Co., a firm specializing in offering guidance from a Christian perspective to professional athletes and celebrities. It is evident from such findings that there is a great need to know how to manage wealth and finances from the poorest of the poor to the wealthiest athletes and celebrities. If money wasn't important, why would it be one of the most talked about subjects mentioned by Jesus, in Proverbs and arguably the whole Bible? We cannot talk about business and its Biblical principles without first understanding why it's so important.

There are many warnings in the Bible about money but there are also many principles. Arguably one of the most well-known verses about money is mentioned by Timothy:

"For the love of money is a root of all the evils; because of this craving, some people have wandered away from the faith and pierced themselves to the heart with many pains." (1 Timothy 6:10 CJB)

Money does not solve all of life's problems. In fact, the Bible says almost quite the opposite, that if you love money, it will likely add sorrows to your life. Interesting how much of America and the world look at money completely differently. Do you ever wonder who first planted that seed of deception in our minds? Perhaps the great deceiver, Satan himself.

Instead of thinking that we are unholy to desire and want to create wealth, it's quite the opposite. Actually, God says He gives us the "ability to create wealth." (Deuteronomy 8:18) He actually encourages us and gives us advice on how to invest (Matthew 25:14–30). God desires for us to have wealth so we can advance His Kingdom. But when we become greedy and horde up earthly treasures for ourselves and chase after the love of money, then we are sure to have many sorrows.

In fact, countless theologians and scholars have debated on what is the most important financial Biblical truth. Many, including Grandich, say the number one most important biblical rule of finance is that *God owns everything*. Grandich says it like this: "You may have bought that house, but He gave you the money to buy it, so it's His." Even your tithe and offering are you giving to Him what He loaned to you in the first place (Malachi 3:8). Nothing you have is yours. Everything belongs to God, including your bank account.

Even as the Proverbs 31 woman considers a field and weighs it before buying, she also weighs the value of her own work. She perceives the value of what she has made and worked hard to create. She doesn't belittle her work. She values it and can calculate its worth unbiasedly. She is aware of her financial hard-won contribution to the household income. Her candle, not going out by night, speaks about her endurance and diligence in her work, even into the late-night hours. She was obviously an early riser as mentioned earlier. She knew how to get things done and would sacrifice when and how it was needed. She woke early when it was required and stayed up late when necessary. She had a "go-getter" attitude of "getting it done." She was capable but knew how to balance her work without burning out. A lot of women burn a candle at both ends, meaning they work really hard without getting the needed and necessary rest or getting self-care. Learning to strike that balance of caring for yourself so you can care for others is a fine art and balancing act. Sometimes you can lose balance and stumble and fall. But then just get back on track.

Remember, it's not about being perfect and "arriving." It's about "becoming perfect" to look more like Jesus every day. It's always about the journey with God and not the destination. Even when we are saved from sin, it's so we can enter into this eternal relationship with God and enjoy the journey of knowing and walking with Him forever. The real destination is the relationship in the process. Jesus worded it well when He said:

"For what shall it profit a man, if he shall gain the whole world, and lose his own soul?" (Mark 8:36 KJV)

If you have the best well-run house and most successful business without a relationship with your own family, then, in a way, you've lost your own soul and the soul of your family. And if you've done all the "right" Proverbs 31 women things without a relationship with God, you've lost the whole point. All of life is the overflow of the relationship with God and His word.

Mary and Martha in the Bible are the best portrayals of this truth. Martha was busy being the "perfect hostess" while Mary was busy being in a relationship with Jesus and loving His company. (Luke 10:38-42) Mary's posture (sitting at the feet of Jesus) was one only a disciple would take (meaning, only men in the day). Martha's insistence that Mary comes help her in the kitchen was frustration that Mary was doing something only men did (learning as a disciple at the feet of a rabbi). But Jesus elevates her and communicates that she has just as much right to be His disciple as a woman as any other of His followers did.

Mary was a friend and disciple of Jesus. You love when a friend does something great for you, but sometimes, you just want them to sit down and spend time with you instead of always doing. God wants us to serve Him diligently and well, but He is always after our hearts first, otherwise, it's a lot of doing and performance without love. Remember 1 Corinthians 13? It says that without love, our speaking is just a loud clanging cymbal and even if we gave all we had to the poor and our bodies to be burned, but didn't have love, it would mean nothing! This is a huge wakeup call, especially when you are powering through your to-do list but haven't spent quality time with the Father. When that happens, you know you've missed what Jesus called "the better thing." That's what He told Martha when she complained that her sister Mary was not helping her in the kitchen. Jesus said Mary had chosen the better thing and it wouldn't be taken from her.

Part of the "quality investments" the Proverbs 31 woman makes is not just financial but the investments she makes for the sake of a relationship. She is wise and intentional and knows her greatest work is the relationship with God first, then her husband, then her children, then her community.

After she sees that her merchandise is good and profitable, she tests a product or business venture and is up late into the night and early in the morning to make her merchandise or business grow. She "gives no sleep to her eyelids" (Proverbs 6: 1-15) because she knows what an increase can mean for her family and for the kingdom of God. She builds her family estate so that "her children can rise up and call her blessed."

But before she can do any of this, she must be perceptive. To perceive something is to be aware and observant. A Proverbs 31 woman doesn't just start a business/career and hopes it's successful. No, she is constantly perceiving if her investment is good or not. Is she making a profit? Is the money and time invested worth her energy? Time away from family? Lack of sleep? No wealth was ever gained without sacrifice of some kind. To be financially independent, you must be perceptive and willing to sacrifice, but at what cost? That's where the Proverbs 31 woman uses her perception.

Even if you have a full-time career, take your profits and invest them to make it grow: a Roth IRA, 401 (K), real estate or even invest in a franchise. The point is this: always grow and invest your earnings into something that yields a return and increase. This may be a trial and error thing if you are not familiar with investing, so start with small investments until you feel safe to make big ones, realizing it's possible to lose all your investment. As the old saying goes, "Nothing ventured, nothing gained."

How many of us would lose sleep over something and invest all our time and energy because we know the joy it will bring? We endure labor pains because of the joy and expectation of where that pain will lead: our newborn baby! Jesus endured the cross because of the joy that was set before Him (Hebrews 12:2). This long-term perspective takes perception to see into the future of what will be or what could be. The same is true with investments. We can endure little sleep because of the joy awaiting us on the other side of our investment of time, energy and effort. We have to trust the process of gaining wealth. Everything worth having in life requires time. A child takes nine months to "bake" before we enjoy its precious little life. Sex, from God's perspective, requires we wait until marriage to enjoy its delights. A raise or job promotion requires proof of talent and time before it is given. If we are patient and allow God time to do His work, we will reap a great reward. As our Dad reminds us, "God doesn't need a lot of time, but He does need some time." It's like us asking God to give us patience — NOW!

As you allow time for your investment to yield its return, you will see a dividend on what you've been working toward. But this does not mean investing in something that is not prosperous. Once you've considered it's worth the investment and it's yielding fruit, then move forward in the confidence of God's word. Constantly be perceiving if your "merchandise is good," and if so, you will be prosperous. It's one of God's principles and His words never return back to Him void (Isaiah 55:11).

Chapter 31
Integrity: The Riches of Knowing Who You Are

"She layeth her hands to the spindle, and her hands hold the distaff." (Prov 31:19 KJV)

There is a Rabbinical saying, "There is no wisdom in a woman but in the distaff," indicating that a woman's great praise is her industry or her work. The spindle and the distaff are the most ancient form of the spinning apparatus which women in ancient Eastern cultures used as their source of income.

The Middle Eastern bride went to her new home amidst rejoicing maidens, the bride's maidens, and attendants would carry in their hands the distaff and the spindle, with brightly colored wools hanging around them. To all who observed, it resounded a message that a woman should resemble a busy bee when it comes to industry. We see this woman being diligent with her hands and not eating the bread of idleness. Her house is not lacking because she doesn't give in to self-indulgence or laziness; rather, she gives of herself to run her household well and uses her gifts to prosper all in her domain. Our great-grandmother said, "A woman should always have her hands busy." Even when she would be reclining in her rocker, she would always have some kind of knitting or crochet work she was doing. The old saying rings true, "Idleness is the devil's playground."

When you look at the word "industry" and its meaning, you realize the Eastern woman was considered a helper in bringing in estate income. A deeper study in Merriam-Webster Dictionary reveals industry to mean: *manufacturing or productive enterprise in a particular field, any general business activity; commercial enterprise; trade or manufacture in general: the ownership and management of companies, factories, etc.: friction between labor and industry. Systematic work or labor, energetic, devoted activity at any work or task; diligence.*

There's an old English proverb that says, "You don't know where you're going until you know where you've been." This is definitely true of the Proverbs 31 woman. It is challenging to know how to live out being a Proverbs 31 woman in the modern day unless we first look at the Proverbs 31 woman of ancient times and study her.

"This is what the Lord says: "Stand at the crossroads and look; ask for the ancient paths, ask where the good way is, and walk in it, and you will find rest for your souls..." (Jeremiah 6:16 NIV)

Upon further study of this ancient woman, you see that she was a seemingly domestic goddess, but she was also a business heroine within her industry. And she was not afraid to walk in that industry because she saw it as a calling from God as a way for her to provide and contribute to the family estate. So, what makes a Proverbs 31 woman different from a feminist? The fact that she honors.

The Apostle Paul instructed the modern women of his day to go back and emulate the ancient matriarchs of the faith (1 Peter 3:5-6). The Proverbs 31 woman honors men. She honors the home, she honors her calling and is not afraid to walk in that. Although there are many good qualities from women's liberation found in the feminist movement, such as equal pay, the right to vote etc., the attitude out of which the feminist movement was birthed from, removes much honor out of a woman's life toward men in her midst. A huge weakness in this movement is the lack of honoring men, often promoting an attitude of finding the joy of putting men in their place or even belittling them. There is a misconception, that by a woman honoring men, she is somehow degrading herself.

We see this with Lucifer, who did not want to honor God through worship. He wanted to put himself above God. This same attitude is often found in the feminist movement. Let us be clear, men and women were created equal before God. (Gen 1:27) Both should be mutually respected and honored by each other. So, we are not saying men deserve more respect than women, but rather, just as much respect as any woman deserves. If we are not careful, we will see the pervasive, modern definition of the feministic attitude creeping into our Christian feminine lives.

There is a Godly kind of "feminism" that the culture does not promote, however. We see this clearly in the many relationships that the Lord Jesus had with women while He was on Earth. He pushed the cultural norms while honoring women to an elevated position that their culture denied them. (John 4:4-26, John 7:53-8-11) We too have been elevated to the highest position as daughters of the King of Kings and Lord of Lords, so the feminist movement in the Christian culture is the liberation of women living out their true freedom as the redeemed of the Lord. According to the word of God, true "feminists" are women who are free to honor men and free to love their enemies and bless those that curse them. This kind of "feminism" brings about the freedom to love and honor men in our midst no matter how they have treated us, knowing that the Father won us to Himself when we were still the enemies of God. What kind of love is this? Unconditional. So, we ought to have this same love. (John 13:34)

Many women gravitate toward feminism, even within the Christian culture, because there they find acceptance and identity. But you don't need to be a feminist to have acceptance. You are fully known and fully accepted in Christ. Only He brings true freedom and liberation!

Women are strong and capable. We have a unique position in which to honor men. A true Proverbs 31 woman uses her position to empower not to deflate. When a woman knows who she is, she is empowered to empower. The best way to fight and avoid the twisted and manipulative attitudes of Lucifer in the world's feminist movement is to know who you are and what you are called to be while understanding how to walk and live that out through the gifts and callings God has placed in you. And that understanding starts as a woman beholds all that she is empowered to be explicitly lined out in Proverbs 31. To learn more about honoring men in a God-given way, we highly recommend the book/Bible study *Love and Respect* by Dr. Emerson Eggerichs.

"A gracious woman attains honor, and ruthless men attain riches." (Proverbs 11:16K NASB)

It is possible to be a woman of honor, a true lady, and businesswoman in one. One does not negate the other. Find your passion and ask yourself, "How can I attain wealth doing what I love?" In doing so, you will live your life out with integrity as the woman God designed you to be.

Chapter 32
Makes and Sells

"She maketh fine linen, and selleth it; and delivereth girdles unto the merchant."
(Proverbs 31:24 KJV)

We see that the Proverbs 31 woman was indeed industrious and willing to work hard to make a profit. As we watch the story evolve of who this woman is, we see her working with wool and flax, and in this verse, we see her making products of fine linen not only for her family but also to sell. She doesn't just sell them herself but she works with merchants so they too can sell her products. She is taking her products and services and getting them into the hands of other people.

In essence, this woman was a fashion designer! She actually created articles of clothing to sell and made them for her business. She was not only diligent in her work but creative at the same time. She had to be up to date on the fashions of the day and made her goods stand out for her business to be profitable. We may not be cloth designers and seamstresses, but we can implement diligence, ingenuity and creativity in whatever our work may be.

We personally know an amazing fashion designer who had some of her own original designs in Vogue magazine and traveled the world buying and selling materials for the design company she worked for. Many people, including some of her colleagues, came to faith in God during her travels. She eventually gave up her six-figure income in obedience to the Lord and is now employed by Him to go and do whatever He bids her to do. She still has a very business-savvy mind and she uses her skill to bless others. This is just part of her ministry now. Eventually, she feels the Lord will take her back into the business arena, but she operates out of obedience to do as God directs. Our sister-in-law also utilizes the principle of "buy and sell." She buys products at a reduced cost and then turns around to sell them online, making a profit. Even though she is a stay-at-home mother, she is still contributing to her family income.

For today, this could include keeping blogs and making money from affiliate marketing or creating your own YouTube channel to teach a skill you have. Blogs and online tutorials are hitting the business world with a bang. It's a new way of selling a service or product. If you give an honest review of something on your blog and someone clicks the link you reviewed and buys the product, you get a commission of that purchase. What could be easier than reviewing products you already use?

Additionally, closer to what the Proverbs 31 woman actually did in selling her own products, you might be better suited to make something to sell online, like on Etsy. By putting your product out there, you are essentially doing what the Proverbs 31 woman did which was to sell her products to the merchants. Even women who sell baked goods at farmer's markets or promotional events are also putting this verse into practice. These are but a few examples of how a modern-day woman could emulate the Proverbs 31 woman. Doing such business ventures sets yourself up for success in other areas of life. By being your own boss, you are in control of your schedule and can prioritize when to work on your business that fits into the family schedule.

And, of course, there are other means you can choose from that would allow you the freedom to live your life by the seven ancient secrets of the Proverbs 31 woman. Whether buying or selling, allow yourself to be led by the Lord in how to use your gifts and calling.

Secret VII: Ministry

"For the LORD your God chose the tribe of Levi out of all your tribes to minister in the LORD's name forever."

(Deuteronomy 18:5 NLT)

Ministry first and foremost is unto the Lord. Yet, like the priests in the Bible, when we minister to God's people, we are ministering to Him. How we live our lives and treat others is a ministry unto the Lord. No matter what you do, if you're a Christian, "ministry" is a part of your everyday life. If you're a mother, you minister daily to the needs of your family. If you're an employee, you minister to your colleagues and coworkers. If you're a businesswoman, you minister to your staff and employees. If you're a woman walking on this Earth, you were designed to be a "help" mate. Some of us have the honor to be a helpmate to our husbands, others in their work and social life, while still others find the balance of managing both. Every Christian, every man, every woman is designed to honor God through their lives and work. In fact, work is our lived-out sacrifice or ministry to God.

Not all labor is quantifiable or measured by a dollar sign. You may not be making a paycheck, but there is a reason Jesus says, "Pray that there would be laborers for the Harvest." (Matthew 9:38) In different seasons of life, some may be laboring for the Lord in ways that do not give a monetary return, yet their labor and work is just as powerful with or without a paycheck.

When the priest would offer sacrifices in the temple to God, they would be "ministering" to Him. There are certain things we do under the heading of ministry, but it is all unto God. Jesus said that when we give a cup of water to one of His children, we are actually giving it to Him. Ministry can be full time work, such as pastors, missionaries, evangelists, etc., or something we do once a week or once a month, such as volunteering at different non-profits or functions, giving donations or financial aid to those in need and going on mission trips or even something as simple as showing hospitality, etc. Ministry is a conscious effort to contribute to and serve the needs of others. The Proverbs 31 woman had a constant awareness of those she was called to minister to, namely her family, and also the poor and needy in her community. Ministry is the mindset of being focused on others.

Chapter 33
Ministry Antennas for the Poor and Needy

"She stretcheth out her hand to the poor; yea, she reacheth forth her hands to the needy." (Proverbs 31:20 KJV)

To stretch out your hand to someone is an intentional action. We have to be deliberate in doing good to others. The Lord knew we had to grow in learning how to do good and show love and kindness to other people. He invites us to labor with Him in doing His work.

He blesses us to be a blessing. Out of our abundance, we can stretch our hand to the poor and give freely. We have been given much so we can, in turn, give to others. It's interesting that this verse makes a distinction between the poor and needy. Poor people refer to someone's financial status, whereas a needy person can refer to any station. So, why does God make a distinction between the two? Because giving to the poor is different than giving to the needy.

The Hebrew definition of the word needy means: "in want, poor." In contrast, the Hebrew meaning for the word poor is: "afflicted, humble, meek." Poor could insinuate financial deficit, while needy could insinuate lack, perhaps financially, materially, emotionally, spiritually or physically. Both are important and the Proverbs 31 woman is concerned with the needs of both.

She gives to the poor. People who are humbled by their poverty and lack are poor. Poor people can be poor financially (which typically is what we think of) or they can be poor and humbled by a recent event in their life. Someone who has just been evicted from their home would be someone who is afflicted. That person would be considered poor. A Proverbs 31 woman has antennas for the poor and is attuned to their needs and outcry for help.

Ellianna: One morning before starting a work session on this book, we were out with a friend. She has such a heart for those in need. As we were driving around, we saw an unusual sight that appeared out of place in our neighborhood: a woman walking with groceries on our street. Unsurprisingly, our friend stopped and asked the lady if she needed a ride. She was attentive to her needs. This is the very essence of a Proverbs 31 woman. Her ministry antennas were up, and she stopped what she was doing to lend a hand. I was not so attentive. In fact, I found myself leaning into "Martha mode," feeling frustrated because our goal was being delayed, the goal of writing this book. I didn't want to be inconvenienced. But the Lord used this experience to kindly show me that five minutes out of our day was not going to hurt the process of completing this book.

"Learn to do good; seek justice, correct oppression; bring justice to the fatherless, plead the widow's cause." (Isaiah 1:17 ESV)

Just as Proverbs 31 woman implements creativity in her business, she brings the same into her ministry outside her business. Let us clarify that she does not separate business from ministry. After all, the Bible says, "Whatsoever you do, do all for the glory of God." (1 Cor 10:31). We are not representing God in compartments. We don't just represent Him when ministering to the poor and needy. We represent Him when we are in the business arena too.

How many times have you been around a successful businessman and saw through the guise of his appearance that he was broken or tormented inside, chained to the approval and acceptance of others, striving to gain respect from his accomplishments? There is a striving worse than death when you are working for acceptance instead of serving because you are already accepted by the only One who counts: God!

There is a difference from being "called" versus being "driven." A good resource on this topic is the book *Ordering Your Private World*. This woman obviously didn't limit her ministry to the business arena alone. She intentionally and purposely sought out the poor and outcast, those pushed to the margins of society. Likewise, we are to minister through our business but also the poor, needy, fatherless and widows.

One year, our mother wanted to reach out to the poor and broken in our community. She was inspired by the book *The Kneeling Christian*, author unknown. She spoke with her church and they agreed they could host a Thanksgiving dinner and a few weeks later, a Christmas dinner at the church gym. The whole church got on board with this and bussed in families in need. We got to cook for them and serve them a hot, warm meal. Everything was decorated beautifully; our mother used her amazing decorating skills to creatively transform the church gym into a winter wonderland with beautiful centerpieces, nice tablecloths and cozy lighting! It was incredible to see the whole church involved. Our dad and older sister Virginia gave a gospel message, and many gave their lives to Jesus. All the children who came received a Christmas gift. It felt like *family* with Christmas songs and carols sung by all. There was so much love and new relationships formed. We got to show the love and heart of the family of God to those who didn't know Him or have a family.

It made a big impact on us as children to see how our mother stepped out in faith to make this happen.

Organizing and rallying the church, friends and family to get behind her idea was no small feat. She intentionally wanted to use her skills to do something for the Lord, to reach out her hand to the poor and needy, even though she was in the throes of child rearing. It was during her personal time with God that she received this idea. From her "prayer closet" with the Father, she got creative and actively did what she felt Him leading her to do. How beautiful!

We each have our own gifts and talents given to us by God for the purpose of showing His glory, creativity and love. Listen to Him, partner with Him, and He will show you what steps to take to actively stretch out your hand to the poor and needy. It doesn't have to be something big and grand. It can be something as simple as having a new acquaintance over for dinner and getting to know them, showing interest in them. You could invite a single person into your home to join your family for dinner, give money to a beggar, pray with them and share with about the hope and love of Jesus.

Melissa: One time I felt led to mail some money to a divorced woman I met in another state. Her name was Dora. She was just coming back to the Lord and she was on my heart. I knew she struggled financially and felt prompted to mail her some money. A day or so after dropping the letter off, it arrived back on my desk at work. "What?" I thought to myself. Then I realized I had forgotten to put a stamp on the envelope. I can't tell you how annoyed and mad I was at myself. I wasn't as grounded in God's goodness and love for me as I am now. All I could see was my lack of attention to stamp the envelope as another big time-waster to my busy day. I knew I had stamps already at home, so I'd have to go back home and get one, then go back to the post office and mail it again. I was extremely busy and when you're really busy, sometimes, the smallest things (that, in reality, don't take much time), seem to take way longer. There I was, all stressed and beating myself up over a stamp. Little did I know the Lord was at work in my seeming forgetfulness. I quickly righted my stamp-less envelope and sent it off again for the second time, double checking everything to make sure all was correct. Not long afterward, I heard from Dora. She was amazed and told me she did not have enough money to pay her rent that month and finally got down on her knees to cry out to God for help. The very next day, my letter arrived with the money that gave her the remaining amount she needed for her rent. She was blown away. I was blown away. I honestly laughed at myself and at how big and awesome God is. It's almost as if He had me forget the stamp on purpose to bring Dora to that place of crying out to Him so He could provide her the money right when she needed it. He cared about her rent getting paid. He cared about me learning that God is bigger than my forgetfulness and not to beat myself up when I'm not perfect.

Sisters, we all need those reminders, don't we? Our whole life is a classroom with the Lord. When we are the ones stretching out our hands to the needy, we receive back more than we could ever give.

In ancient times, since the culture was male-dominant, a woman who was widowed was left without the protection of a man and did not have the normal cushion of his added income to support. She was much more vulnerable than a widowed woman today; being left without a husband, however, no matter what time in history, widowhood can leave a woman more vulnerable, emotionally or financially. Likewise, an orphan, in ancient times and today, is just as vulnerable and susceptible to the evils they would be protected from in a strong family unit.

"Pure and undefiled religion in the sight of our God and Father is this: to visit orphans and widows in their distress, and to keep oneself unstained by the world." (James 1:27 NASB) In essence, the Lord is highlighting the vulnerable and helpless as the ones we are to seek out. An unwanted child in the womb is most vulnerable of all. They can't speak up for themselves and they sure can't run away from danger. Some of the other most vulnerable in our world are the men, women and children bound in the sex slave industry. It's abusive and forced slavery that not only gives physical harm to the enslaved but also mental and emotional havoc. The Lord feels strongly about the helpless and listens to their cries for help: *"He gives justice to the oppressed and food to the hungry. The LORD frees the prisoners."* (Psalm 146:7 NLT)

May we learn to do good. May we learn to love as Jesus loved. May we learn to walk the walk and not just talk the talk. Stand up for the helpless and be a voice for the voiceless. Extend your hand to the poor, needy and vulnerable, whatever that looks like in your life and however the Lord leads you. He just needs our availability, not our perfection.

"Dear children, let us not love with words or speech but with actions and in truth." (1 John 3:18 NIV)

Chapter 34
Reaping What You Sow: Honest Praise of a Child Tells All

"Give her of the fruit of her hands; and let her own works praise her in the gates."
(Proverbs 31:31 KJV)

Growing up with six other siblings, it was evident to us that children were a blessing. Our mother had several helpers to help keep the home, prepare meals, do chores, prep for parties, babysit and the list goes on. "Many hands make the load light" was one of our mother's favorite sayings. With so many children, it was a challenge to keep a tidy home. Like any mother, this was frustrating to her. Yet she would always let us know that she would rather have an unkempt home for a few hours a day (before we did our chores), with lots of children, than have a clean home with no children. She would often quote, *"Where there are no oxen, the manger is empty, but from the strength of an ox come abundant harvests."* (Proverbs 14:4 NIV) This is an analogy that children provide great strength even though they may be messy at times.

The works of a mother are never-ending. The greatest role of a mother, when it comes to her children, is that of a teacher. And one of the best ways to teach children is by example. Our mother taught us how to keep a home, how to live by priorities, how to host, how to be gracious, how to respect men, how to be honoring to a husband, and the list goes on. She taught all this by doing and exemplifying. Deuteronomy 11:19 says teaching our children should be a lifestyle: *"Teach them [God's law] to your children, talking about them when you sit at home and when you walk along the road, when you lie down and when you get up."*

In essence, teaching should never stop, it's just a part of life. In so doing, you take time to teach by example. Even a simple act of apologizing to your children when you make a mistake is teaching your children, too. Everything you do in life can be an avenue to teach, if you allow it. By living a life like this, your children will watch, observe and learn. And eventually (though maybe not right now), they will praise you for the example and heritage you leave them. A mother can set an example in many ways, how she gives her time and resources, how she works, how she disciplines, how she counsels, how she serves, how she loves and so on.

For those who have a mother still living, you are blessed. We all know moms and even dads or spouses who aren't perfect, but if you still have a mother, to praise her is your unique way to honor her for all the good works she has done. Listen up, we could all talk about things our mothers could do differently, but the fact is, no mom (or parent for that matter) is perfect, but they were perfectly crafted for us to make us the women we needed to be. Yes, even smothering mothers, bossy mothers, old fashioned mothers, not-there-for-me mothers, whatever type of mother you had, God chose that mom for you. One definition of honor by Pastor Bill Johnson of Bethel Church, Redding, California is "celebrating who a person is without stumbling on who they are not." As Scripture says, "Honor your father and mother." This is the first commandment with a promise." (Ephesians 6:2 NLT) "That promise being a long life." (Exodus 20:12)

Of course, honor is a choice we can all make or chose not to make. And whatever difficulty you may have (or have had) with your mom, know that "[*God*] *works all things together for good to those who are the called according to his purpose.*" (Romans 8:28 KJV) It's time we lay our pride aside and rebuild broken relationships. Even if your mother gave you up for adoption, you can still be grateful that she chose life. Ladies, can we be honest here for a moment? It's our mothers we're talking about. At the very least, thank them for laying down their lives for you, (the greatest form of love, John 15:13) to bring you into the world.

Love is a choice. We have a choice to choose whether or not to love our mothers. And that choice often starts with gratitude and being thankful for all they've done for us — whether big or small. They've made sacrifices for you. Isn't that why we love Christ, because He died and laid down his life for us?

If you already have a great relationship with your mom, good for you. For those who want a better relationship, start by naming the things you admire and appreciate about your mother. What are you grateful for concerning your mother? Did she provide food for you to eat, a bed to sleep in? Did she lay her life down to bring you into the world? Did she give you advice that, had you listened, would have been beneficial? Did she encourage or help pay for sports or music lessons? We encourage you to write down all the things your mother did that you can be grateful for. What sacrifices did she make on your behalf? Make a list and turn it into a thank you card and watch if you get the desired response. If not, you have still praised her for all the work she has done and in doing so, have praised her "in the gates," which is a public place. You may even consider writing something on social media (a public place) about what you appreciate about your mom.

The week leading up to Mother's Day, there are signs everywhere to remind people to show honor to mom and remember to do something special for her. We're glad our culture recognizes mothers and chose a day out of each year to honor them. Even if you had a drug-addicted mom, you still had a mom. Many children in foster care have said they'd rather have an absent mom than none at all. If you have a mom, let her know she is loved and appreciated. In some way that feels genuine and honest. She does deserve at least a thank you. Your mom is not you, you are not her, but maybe you both have made each other what you are today. She couldn't be a mother without you and you certainly wouldn't be here without her. Are there things you wish your mom did differently? Did those frustrating things make you a better person? Thank her for that.

"Finally, brothers and sisters, whatever is true, whatever is noble, whatever is right, whatever is pure, whatever is lovely, whatever is admirable—if anything is excellent or praiseworthy—think about such things." (Philippians 4:8 NIV)

If your mother is no longer living, you can still honor her by speaking of her good qualities, perhaps to your own children, instead of speaking negatively of her. We are not encouraging blindness to a person's faults but rather making a willful choice to focus more on their positive qualities than their negative ones.

It's like a sheet of white paper with a black dot in the middle; we have a decision to focus on the black dot or the white part around the black dot. We have been there, wanting to focus on all the ugly faults of a person and just get stuck in seeing them in their muck. *"LORD, if you kept a record of our sins, who, O Lord, could ever survive?"* (Psalm 130:3 NIV)

When we focus on other's faults, often the fear of God will come on us quickly, knowing the way we treat others is how we will be treated. If we only judge others based on their weaknesses, we are giving permission to be judged by that same standard. This verse has liberated us to depend on the grace and goodness of our God and focus on how we should forgive and move forward with others who have mistreated or deeply hurt us. There's no freedom without forgiveness; because we have been totally forgiven, we have been liberated to forgive others just as He has forgiven us.

"For in the same way you judge others, you will be judged, and with the measure you use, it will be measured to you." (Matt 7:22 NIV)

If, perhaps you never knew your mother, honor the person who stepped into that role and was like a mother to you. We can't always choose other's actions toward us, but we can always choose our response. To praise someone is a choice we make. What will you choose from this day forward?

Chapter 35
Love: Your Highest Priority

"And now these three remain: faith, hope and love. But the greatest of these is love." (I Corinthians 13:13 NIV)

We should always do good and help all those who are needy, but the Bible tells us especially to those who belong to the household of faith, meaning all believers (Galatians 6:10). Help those in need, give to the poor and needy, but if you are more willing to help those outside your own spiritual family instead of those in need within the household of faith, according to God, you are worse than an infidel. (1 Timothy 5:8) Although this verse is talking about your physical birth family, we believe the same principle can apply to our spiritual family as well.

We don't always get recognized for helping those inside our church or our community. We don't get recognized for bringing someone a casserole after they've had surgery and can't move. But God notices. The world will notice when you give large amounts of time or money to those who aren't Christians because that's a "good thing." And it is a good thing — keep doing that. God calls us to give and help others when there is an opportunity to do so. Don't ignore one to do the other. And, certainly, don't forget about those who are in your immediate family. We are also instructed to bear one another's burdens and in doing so, we "Fulfill the law of Christ." (Galatians 6:20). What is the law of Christ? We learned about the law of kindness earlier. We know the greatest commandment God gave was to love your neighbor as yourself. In essence, therefore, the Proverbs 31 woman's whole life is based on *love.*

She spends time with God because she loves Him. She tends to herself and her needs to be there for her family because she loves them. She tends to the ways of her husband because she loves him. She teaches because she loves others and wants what is best for them. She is involved in business because she loves her community and family and wants to support her children's estate because she loves them and wants to provide for their needs even when she is gone. She knows a wise person leaves an inheritance for their children's children (Proverbs 13:22). She gives to the poor and needy out of love and out of the abundance of her wealth. In the end, a Proverbs 31 woman is able to do all the above and balance all these amazing things because she is motivated by love.

If you feel overwhelmed by all we've discussed and the priorities we're supposed to live your lives by, start with this: live your life based on love. Choose relationships over tasks. Turn worried thoughts into prayers and then receive a heart at rest. Out of love, Christ died for our sins and bore the transgressions of the world. He was beaten and bruised because He *loved* us. Out of love, we give birth, even though it's not an enjoyable experience, because we know, as women, Godly offspring is one of the greatest gifts we can give to the world. Start your first day toward being a Proverbs 31 woman with this declaration:

Proverbs 31 Declaration:

I declare from this day forward to purpose in my heart to live according to the principles outlined in God's word and specifically for me as a woman in Proverbs 31. I will choose God first in all I do and seek to live according to His ways and laws. Namely, I choose the path of love, living each day to esteem others (my husband, family, friends, colleagues and God) above myself. I commit to serve because greatest in the kingdom of heaven are those who serve and lay down their lives for others. I offer my body as a living sacrifice and a holy temple, both before and after marriage. I purpose to do my husband good all the days of my life and, through God's grace, commit to keep my body holy and set apart for my husband and my Bridegroom, Lord Jesus Christ.

If God blesses my body with children, I will commit to bear and raise them in the ways of the Lord. I say *no* to self and laziness and say *yes* to God and His way of love, knowing that what seems right in my eyes may not always be what's right in His eyes. I commit to make sacrifices where needed to support my husband and family. God knew men needed a lot of help so He made all of us women to be their helpmate.

I commit to take care of myself so I can take care of my family and be there for them, full of energy. If I'm out of shape, I purpose by the grace of God to do something about that. *I will* make a change. This I purpose and declare in my heart to do before God and a witness. I commit to be involved with my family estate by researching and learning ways to create wealth and a lasting inheritance for my children's children. I purpose to strive to live my life by priorities making time to raise my children as Godly leaders for the next generation, teaching them to observe all that God commanded by leading out a Godly life committed to the ways of the Lord.

I commit to not put "ministry" above the needs of my family (which is my own little missionary training ground). If I am single, I commit to not put "ministry" above relationships. I commit to live my life by priorities: God, Personal, Husband, Home (Family), Teacher, Business and Ministry. In so doing, I commit to order my ways aright. I start afresh and anew today with the Lord by my side.

Your Signature: _____

Witness Signature: _____

Salvation Prayer

Jesus Christ came to earth and paid the penalty for our sins so that He could invite us into a personal relationship with Him (John 3:16). Without a relationship with Jesus Christ, life and this book really have no meaning. Do you have a personal relationship with Him? Would you like to make a decision today to live this moment forward under the Lordship of Jesus and walk a life according to His Word and principles? If so, then God says:

"If you declare with your mouth, 'Jesus is Lord,' and believe in your heart that God raised Him from the dead, you will be saved. For it is with your heart that you believe and are justified, and it is with your mouth that you profess your faith and are saved." (Romans 10:9-10 NIV)

To give your life to Him and enter this relationship with Jesus as Lord and Saver of your life requires us to turn away from our sinful lives and enter into a new creation of walking and living our lives according to the God's word: the Bible. If you feel you understand this and are ready to declare your faith in Him, we invite you to say this prayer out loud:

Lord God, I know I have sinned against You and confess my unrighteousness to you. I believe in my heart and confess with my mouth that Jesus Christ is Lord and that You raised Him from the dead. I want to enter into a relationship with You. I give my life to You and invite Your Son, Jesus Christ, to come into my life. I give my heart to You, Jesus, and choose to receive Your gift of salvation. Save me. You are now Lord and Savior of my life.

Amen

Sign:_____ Date:_____

After you've prayed this prayer, there will no doubt be times when you'll struggle if you're actually saved. Return to this page and see the date you confessed Jesus as Lord whenever Satan tempts you that you are not saved. We encourage you to get a Bible and start reading it daily and get involved in a community of believers. A church is a great place to start to find this fellowship.

We have already been praying for you. If you have prayed this prayer and made the decision of choosing Jesus as Lord and Savior of your life, congratulations! We are now sisters in Christ. We would love to hear from you and continue to lift you up in prayer and rejoice with you in your new life. Email us at: womenarisingbook@gmail.com.

About the Authors:

Ellianna and Melissa are sisters who grew up in a large family in Arkansas. They both own their own businesses and are involved with non-profits. They spent three years on the mission field with their family growing up. Ellianna, the elder sister, is a mother of one and wife to Ben Temple. They reside in Little Rock, AR.

Ellianna is an etiquette and lifeskill coach. She founded Courtesy First, a company that teaches the value of Courtesy and manners in both the workplace and life. She is also heavily involved with a non-profit called Water for Christ, which drills water wells in developing countries while also sharing the gospel.

Melissa lives in Little Rock, Arkansas and is a Massage Therapist. She founded New Hope Massage. She is heavily involved with the non-profit "Operation Exodus" which helps with humanitarian aid for Jewish people and assists with Aliyah (their return back to Israel from the nations).

All along their many travels in life, both sisters have always had a heart for other woman and the unique challenges presented to them in today's society. Seeing the need both nationally and internationally for answers of how to live, how to prioritize life's many challenges, how to handle money, love, relationship with God and more, they both felt lead to write this book to answer many of the questions and challenges women face today. Get a cup of tea and sit with Ellianna and Melissa and journey back in time to learn the seven Ancient Secrets found in the life of the Proverbs 31 woman to live out today.

References

"Quiet Time: A Practical Guide for Daily Devotions"

"Intercessory Prayer" Dutch Sheets.

"George Muller: The Guardian of Bristol's Orphans." Janet and Geoff Benge

"The Total Money Makeover" Dave Ramsey's Book

"Tortured for Christ," Richard Wurmbrand

"Confessions of a Wall Street Whiz Kid." Peter Grandich

"Love and Respect." Dr. Emerson Eggerichs

"The Kneeling Christian" Author unknown.

"A Praying Wife" Elizabeth George

"Ordering Your Private World" Gorden McDonald

"How to Win Friends and Influence People" Dale Carnegie

Hidden Keys to Loving Relationships Gary Smalley

Learn More

Facebook: WomenArising - @WomenArisingBook

Instagram: @WomenArisingBook - #WomenArisingMovement

Website: WomenArisingBook.com

Speaking Engagements: womenarisingbook@gmail.com

Please leave a review of Women Arising book on Amazon.

Acknowledgment Page

Special thanks to the people listed below for their contributions to this book. Thank you for your belief and your support.

Jo and Kevin McCray

Partners Against Trafficking Humans (PATH) & Louise Allison

Pastor and Mrs. John Temple

Rachel Gilchrist

Benjamin Temple

Mary Maude Shafer

Diane and Jason Temple

Emily McCray

Susan Reasoner

Erin Sanders